BE A MAN!

Be a Man!

Becoming the Man God
Created You to Be

By Father Larry Richards

IGNATIUS PRESS   SAN FRANCISCO

Cover art:
Photograph © istockphoto / Nick Schlax
Author photo by Paul Lori

Cover design by Roxanne Mei Lum

©2009 Ignatius Press, San Francisco
All rights reserved
ISBN 978-1-58617-403-3
Library of Congress Control Number 2009924213
Printed in the United States of America ∞

CONTENTS

INTRODUCTION

We always remember the last words that people say to us before they die, especially the last words of someone we loved. These words resonate throughout our minds and affect our lives in a lasting way. This is especially true of the last words of advice of a loving father to his son. King David knew this as he was talking to his son Solomon and was giving him his final advice before he was "to go the way of all the earth." David looks at Solomon and says, "Take courage and be a man" (1 Kings 2:2 [RNAB]).

David knew that if his son was going to be a great leader, then he would have to first be a great man. This book is about being the kind of man that each of us was created to be. To do this does not require perfection. For David most certainly was not perfect—he was a murderer, an adulterer, and the list goes on; but he was a man who knew who he was and strove with all his being to be better.

Yes, David was weak and filled with many things that we might not respect, but God says of him, "I have found in David, the son of Jesse, a man after my heart, who will do all my will" (Acts 13:22). Many of us can relate to David (well, at least I know I can!), and from the distant past he encourages us to be men who do God's will.

In the past forty years or so, you may have noticed that some of the women have become more masculine and some of the men more feminine. Some of us seem to be confused, going against the way we were created: "So God created man in his own image, in the image of God he created him; male and female he created them" (Gen 1:27). There is a difference! Men are not called to be women and vice versa. This has caused more problems than we can deal with here; but we are different—not better, but different—and we are called to be fully men!

This book will focus on the biblical perspective concerning what it is to be a man. Therefore, we will use the following for our role models: King David from the Old Testament, St. Paul from the New Testament, and Jesus—the Alpha and Omega of all men.

It is Jesus Christ Himself Who reveals to us what it is to be a man. He was a man for others; He gave Himself away. He challenged people, He loved people, He was strong, and He died for others—and He commanded His disciples to do the same.

And so that is what this book is going to be about. It's about giving away our lives. It's about taking the one life God has given to us and giving it away. What you are being invited to do is to die for others, in the sense of putting others' needs above your own. Aren't you excited? But to be like Christ, and to be like all the great men, this will cost you your life.

Each chapter ends with tasks that must be accomplished and questions to reflect on and discuss. I would encourage you to read this whole book in its chronological order, for each chapter builds upon the previous one. If you commit yourself now to read the whole book and accomplish the tasks, then I promise you that your life will be changed forever.

So, are you ready? This is not the time to be a wimp. Today the world needs real men! Your family is counting on you; your friends are counting on you; your world is counting on you; your God is counting on you—so don't be afraid: take courage and be a man!

CHAPTER 1

Be a Man Who Stays Focused on the Final Goal

Call no man happy before his death, for by how he ends, a man is known.

—Sirach 11:28 (RNAB)

You are going to die!

Nice way to start a book, huh? I know, but I want you to let this thought sink in: You are going to die. This is the truest reality there is. This is what makes us all the same. It doesn't matter how rich we are, or how popular we are, or how powerful we are: we are all going to "kick the bucket" one day. Isn't that a nice thought?

Okay, you may say, so what? After we come to accept this basic reality, we have to make sure we do everything with our end in mind. God tells us in the Book of Sirach, "Call no man happy before his death, for by how he ends, a man is known" (11:28 [RNAB]). The world is filled with examples of men who began well and ended badly! We need to make sure that we are not one of them!

If we keep our end in mind then we can begin to reflect on what is most important: What will I accomplish with my short time on earth? What do I want people to say about me once I've taken my last breath? Was my life worth living? Will I be a person who changed the world? Will I be a person who gave more than I took? Or will I be a person who took more than I gave? Will people say of me, "I loved to be around that man because he was a true man and he gave his life away for others"? Or will they say, "That person was one of the most miserable human beings you would ever want to meet"? What will others say about you?

Recently I had a friend pass away. He was seventy years old, and a monsignor in the Catholic Church. He was a large man, and a good man, but he also had a fiery temper. As the bishop preached the funeral homily he said, "Monsignor was a man who had a generous heart, and he served the people with all his heart—sometimes with a smile, and sometimes with a growl." This man was not perfect, but daily he gave his life away.

What will the people who talk at your funeral say about you?

What we have to do is take some time to sit and meditate about taking our last breath. What do you want your wife to say about you? What do you want your kids to say about you? Or the people you work with? What do you want the people you just met to say? After you take some time in thought and prayer, write down what you want others to say about you and then start to make that your goal. Once you've decided, "Okay, when I am taking my last breath this is what I want", you can start living your life with your end goal in mind. You will start living in such a way that when the day of your death happens, the people who know you will say what you want them to say.

I have thought about this a lot in my own life. I was a typical blue-collar family child who grew up in Pittsburgh, Pennsylvania, with no real religion in my life. My father was a city of Pittsburgh police officer, and my mother also later became a police officer; some thought that I would follow in their footsteps, and in some ways I guess I did.

My mother was Catholic in name, but didn't go to church much. She thought that the Church kept people away from God. She thought, "Oh, you do something bad or are in a bad marriage, then you cannot go to church." Although my mother saw the Church as keeping people away from God, it was my father who had the most interesting theology. My dad, my dear father, believed in the God of the Old Testament, the one that gave us the Ten Commandments. He believed that Jesus Christ was God's Son, but that Jesus changed the rules a little too much. Jesus said, "You have heard that it was said, 'An eye for an eye and a tooth for a tooth.' But I say to you, Do not resist one who is evil. . . . Love your enemies and pray for those who persecute you" (Mt 5:38, 39, 44). So my dad believed that although Jesus Christ was the Son of God, God the Father got mad at Him and had Him killed because Jesus changed all the rules. Quite an interesting theology! You think your family was dysfunctional? This is just the beginning of stories about my family—we all come from some kind of dysfunctional family. More on this in the next chapter!

As I grew up, religion was not really part of my family life; but my parents did send me to a Catholic school, and so I did have some religious influence. I was not a horrible teenager but I drank like the other youth. One thing that I never did was take illegal drugs, because my police officer father once threatened me: "If I ever catch you drinking, I will punish you but I will understand; *but* if I ever catch you taking drugs—I will kill you!" I believed him! That is why to this very day, and he has been dead a long time, I've never tried any drugs. I still think he would come back and kill me. I did everything else, though.

I was a trouble-making son of a cop, and, in my day, cops' kids were the worst youth because we could get away with just about anything. All my friends got arrested except for me because of who my dad and my mother were.

I dated and had great girlfriends and did everything else that teens do. I thought that I would be a draftsman or a police officer or whatever else that I liked. I thought that I would marry and have ten kids—yes, ten—nine boys and a baby girl! I was just doing my own thing and thinking that life is just life and you have to make the best of it.

Everything changed for me one day as I sat in my English class during my junior year in high school. We were reading the play *Our Town*, a three-act play by Thornton Wilder. It is a pretty simple play, but it had a not-so-simple impact on my life at the time. At the end of the play one of the main characters, Emily Webb, dies. While in the graveyard with the other people who are dead there, she asks them if she could go back and relive a day in her life; she is reluctant to do so but decides to anyway. Emily decides to revisit her twelfth birthday. Here she realizes how fast time flies and how we take so much for granted.

The play encourages people to really live life and not to miss the little things. But what hit me as a seventeen-year-old kid was that I was going to die one day. And it scared the hell, literally, right out of me. I started to shake in class and to sweat; I began thinking: "Oh my God, I am going to die. I am going to die! So what is the meaning of life? Is there any meaning? Is there anything after death?"

Death is the ultimate thing that takes control out of our hands. Even if we commit suicide, we cannot control what happens after we die. Not one of us had control over our own birth and not one of us has control of what happens after we die.

I hate that! As a man I love to be in control! I don't know if any of you can relate, but I like to be in charge.

When I am in control of things, I can determine, or at least influence, the outcome. I like that.

That is why I am not a big flier. If I were flying the plane, that would be fine, but I have to trust someone else. I hate that! Here I am, thirty-five thousand feet in the air, and someone else has total control of my life!

That is what death is, isn't it? The truth is that we cannot even take our next breath without God saying okay. While you are reading this book, a plane could be flying over where you are reading and all of a sudden you hear "putt . . . putt . . . putt . . . bang" and the plane comes crashing on top of you. You're dead—that fast. You are not even in control of your next breath; that is how dependent you are!

When I sat there and realized for the first time at seventeen that I was going to die, my next thought was, "God, I don't believe in anything." I suddenly realized that fifty years before, I didn't exist. Some of you may have already realized this but I didn't. It was hard for me to imagine that the world existed before I existed! Not only that, but it went on quite well without me. It will go on quite fine one hundred years from now without me also. Without believing in anything, I figured that I was in oblivion before I was born and that when I die I was going to go back into nothingness. That's all. The world existed a million years before me, and it will exist after me.

I knew I needed to believe in something, but why should I believe anything just because that was the way I was brought up? I thought, "Okay, I've got to find out what's real." I am not going to believe in something just because my parents happen to be Catholic and Protestant and happen to have had me baptized. I could have been brought up Muslim or Buddhist or atheist. Just because you are taught something, that doesn't make it true. I wanted to know "What is true? What is real? Is God real; does He exist?" I needed to find out for myself.

At the time, when I was seventeen years old, in Pittsburgh I was working in what was called the U.S. Steel Building. Each day I would walk from the U.S. Steel Building to the Church of the Epiphany, next to what is now called the Mellon Arena. I would enter that beautiful church and kneel there and ask God, "Do You exist? Don't You exist? Do You care? Don't You care?" I went there almost every weekday for many months. I was seeking, but at first I did not find anything or anybody—nothing. Nothing!

One day, though, I was watching TV. Now when I was a kid, and some of you can relate to this, we didn't have remote controls and we didn't have cable in Pittsburgh. Maybe other people did, but my house did not. My television had four stations. We had the three networks and sometimes we got the WQED on VHF. I'd have to sit real close to the TV so I could turn the stations. Back then, there were not many interesting programs on the four stations. But one day as I was watching TV, clicking through the channels trying to find something to watch, I turned past a Billy Graham Crusade. As soon as I saw who it was I thought, "Oh no, Billy Graham! Click off!" But right before I clicked Billy Graham off I heard him say: "I've seen people die!" and then I turned to another channel and then I thought, "Well, let's hear what he has to say", and so I clicked him back on. Billy said again: "I've seen people die. And some people when they are dying are so afraid they cry, 'I'm afraid. I don't want to die. I don't want to die. I'm afraid. Please help me! I'm afraid.'" Then, he said, "And I have watched other people die, and they are smiling from ear to ear saying, 'Jesus, I'm coming home.'" I remember thinking, "Boy, if you could face death with no fear, that would be the greatest gift you could ever have—to be able to face death with no fear." I needed to know if God was real or not.

I went back to the Church of the Epiphany, knelt down, and tried again: "God, do You exist? Don't You exist? Do You care? Don't You care?" Finally, one day, after about six months—sitting there in the church, kneeling, seeking, and just crying out to God—I came to know that Jesus Christ was real and that He was God! How did Christ reveal Himself to me? As I knelt there I became aware that I was not alone. Here before me was the God of the universe, Who had always been there, but I was so focused on myself that I could not see Him. I did not hear His voice at first but I felt His Presence. A Real Presence. A Presence that keeps everything in existence! I remember looking at Him and saying, "Lord, whatever You want I will do." So at seventeen years old while sitting in the Church of the Epiphany, I heard the Lord tell me: "I want you to be a priest." My life was about to change—a lot!

This was not going to be an easy task, as I soon found out. I went to the pastor of the local parish; but since my family never went to church, he laughed at me. He would not recommend me to to go to seminary. My friends thought that I was crazy; one of my friends said to me, "I will bet that you will never become a priest—you like girls too much!" God sure proved them all wrong, on the first part anyway!

Why do I share with you this story? Because the "God question" is the question that you will have to deal with before you can move on. Do you know that God exists? If not, what are you doing to find out if He is real or not? Let me help you. Read on.

How did I know in that moment that God was talking to me? How did I know that Jesus is more real than anything else? These are the same questions that I start my retreats with when I talk to high school students. For example, I once did a retreat for fifteen hundred boys at a Catholic high school in the South. It was a Monday morning at eight o'clock, and there was a full school assembly. These kids were not very excited to have a priest coming to talk to them during their first period on a Monday morning.

I walked into this big gym and found that some of the kids were already sleeping and the others were disgusted with whoever invited me to come. The first thing I said to them was, "Gentlemen, I submit to you that Jesus Christ is not God."

A few of them perked up. "Huh? Is that a priest who just said that?"

Again I said: "I submit to you that He is not God, gentlemen. You prove to me that He is", I continued.

They took that bait real fast, so I just started picking on different youth.

"You, do you believe Jesus Christ is God?" I asked, pointing toward a boy.

"Yeahhhh!"

"Why do you believe?" I pressed.

"Because the Bible says so, Father", he replied with a nice, self-assured smile on his face.

"Ooooooohhh, the Bible says so", I said. I then continued, "Muslims have a Bible and it doesn't say Jesus Christ is God. Jewish people have a Bible that doesn't say Jesus Christ is God. Mormons have a Bible that says Jesus is a god. There are many Bibles out there. What makes our Bible right?"

"Uh oh", the first kid let out; so I looked at another kid and asked, "You, do believe Jesus Christ is God?"

"Yeah."

"Why?"

The biggest answer you always get is, "I don't know. I don't know." That is where most people are. Most kids don't know, either. In truth, if you go into a church and ask people if they believe that Jesus is God and then ask why, they will say they don't know either. It's how they were brought up.

At these retreats I always get one smart aleck that says, "No! I don't believe Jesus is God", to which I'll respond, "Okay, enjoy hell!" Everyone laughs. Now of course I am not saying that the kid is going to hell; I am trying to get the boys' attention so that they know that our decisions have consequences!

Anyway, I moved on to the next person: "Do you believe Jesus Christ is God?"

"Yes", the boy said.

"Why?" I asked.

"He performed miracles, Father."

"Ooooooohhh! But, Benny Hinn performs miracles too", I said.

(Do you ever see Benny Hinn on TV? Benny Hinn will ask, "Are you ready?" "We're ready!" the crowd will shout back. "Are you really ready?" "We're really ready." Then, he'll raise his hands over the crowd and all the people start to fall; it is like a spiritual wave! They all drop to the ground. Some people say that's a miracle.)

Sometimes a young boy will say, "He died for us, Father, come on."

"Ooooooohhh. Is all I have to do is die for you? I am going to die anyway. Why not die for you, if I get to be God out of it? I'll do that. Sure, why not?"

Finally, after everything they say and I completely blow each answer out of the water, and I have managed to get them all mad at me, they look at me and say, "Okay, no matter what we say you are going to say we're wrong."

Every once in a while, though, someone gets the answer right, to a degree. I'll say, "Okay, son, do you believe He is God?"

"I do."

"Why?"

"Because He rose from the dead, Father." Ding, ding, ding, ding, ding!

"How do you know He rose from the dead?"

"The Bible says so", he'll say, going back to the old standby answer. Then, everyone laughs.

Once the boys are thoroughly confused, and frustrated, I'll finally say, "Come on; now ask me."

"Okay. Father, do you believe Jesus Christ is God?"

"I do", I'll say.

"Why?" they all shout at once, just waiting to shoot down my answer like I shot down theirs.

"Because I know Him; I've experienced Him. Every day of my life since I was seventeen years old, I've spent an hour a day, minimum, with the God of the universe. I would die for Him; I would die for Him in an instant. He is the most important thing in my life. I know Him."

See, that is what it ultimately comes down to. What about you? Where are you at with this God, because that is the ultimate question, men! Does God exist? Doesn't He exist? Is Christ God? Isn't He God? Is there life after death? Is there not? Is this all a waste of time or is this all for a purpose? What is the purpose of life?

In the Catholic tradition, we have been taught the meaning of life from the old Baltimore Catechism, a meaning which is now being taught in the universal Catechism, the *Catechism of the Catholic Church*. To the question, "Who made me?" the Church teaches us to respond, "God made me." The next question is, "Why did God make me?" and the answer is, "God made me to know Him, love Him, and serve Him in this world, so that I can be happy with Him in the next."

In my tradition the first meaning and purpose of life is to know God! Not know about God, but to know God. So the question for you right now is: "Do you know God? Do you know Him intimately like you know your wife; or like you know your best friend; or your children? Do you know Jesus Christ?" If the answer in your heart of hearts is, "No, I haven't a clue", then you haven't even begun, yet to live, the purpose of your life. You haven't even begun!

As I said earlier, you have to deal with the question of whether God exists, and, if He does, do you *know* that He exists? It is the most important question of your life. If you do know Jesus, then you know the joy that He gives you. If you do not know Him, then it is going to take you time, but well worth the time that it will take you!

How do you fall in love with someone? Those of you who are married, you know that you did not get to know your future wife by meeting her once and giving her forty-five minutes to an hour once a week. You spent time with her. You got to know her. If you are not married, how did you become friends with your very best friend? The number one way friendship grows, gentlemen, is through time spent with one another. The same is true with our relationship with God. It might take you months—it might take you years—but you have to do it. You have to keep spending time with God until the answer to the question of whether or not *you* know God is unequivocally yes.

I tell people to always seek truth because truth will always lead you to God. The problem is too many people just are not interested in seeking truth. They just live for today; they never think about what might happen tomorrow. Others think they know truth, because they were taught something and they just believe it because they were taught it. Others are afraid that if they open their minds to something other than what they think they already believe then they will live their lives in fear. If something is really true, then you do not have to be afraid of anything else. If what you believe cannot handle truth, then what you believe isn't true. God is the ultimate truth. He can take any kind of doubt. He can handle it. He can take your doubts.

Everything I believed, I first doubted—everything. I doubted first, then I spent time pleading with God, "You've got to reveal this to me, Lord." We get our strength to become real men when we look to the God of the universe, Who created you and me, and admit that we need Him to find the answers we seek.

Now this is *much* more than just going through the motions of a relationship with God! You can know a lot about God, and do a lot of things for God, but when you enter into a relationship with God it will cost you your life—period. This is what love is about. Most people never get this far. Are you man enough to seek God more than anything?

Most men are willing to spend time doing just about anything else—make money, work out, watch sports, etc.—rather than spend time getting to know God. I used to teach boys at an all-boys Catholic high school. The main argument every year was, what is more important—God or sports? What do you think won? Sports! Sports can become a god for people because, many times, people give so much of their time and energy to sports. Every year I'd have the same conversation.

"Gentlemen, what do you want to do this year?" I'd ask.

"We are going to be state champions, Father", my *Catholic school* students would reply.

"Whoa, state champions. I'm impressed. What are you going to do, gentlemen, to become state champions?"

Do you know what they would say? They will have to spend four hours a day, every day, throwing a football, kicking a soccer ball, or hitting a hockey puck; the swimmers will have to wake up at 4:30 in the morning to start swimming—and they did it. They still do it to this day, so they can become state champions. They did it gladly. Can you imagine?

Years ago, the football team actually became the state champions! Those kids were on the top of the world! "Look at us, we're state champions." A lot of them went to college and received full scholarships. But, now, they are doing nothing when it comes to sports. Nothing! When they get to be my age, they will tell their sons, "When I was your age, son, I was a state champion football player." And their kids will look at them and say, "Shut up, Dad. You are just fat and bald now—nobody cares."

People put all this time and energy into things that are passing and ultimately will not matter. If I asked those same kids, "Gentlemen, what are you going to do this year?"

"We are going to be state champions."

"What are you going to do to prove to me you are going to be state champions?"

If they say, "Well, we are going to practice once a week, if we feel like it, for forty-five minutes to an hour and we are going to have good thoughts about the game."

I would say: "Wrong answer, gentlemen. You are going to be horrible in sports. You are not going to go anywhere if you give it only forty-five minutes to an hour and add some good thoughts."

Yet, with those same types of kids, every year I walk in and say, "Gentlemen, do you want to go to heaven?"

"Yes, Father!" they say.

"What are you going to do to prove to me, gentlemen, that you want to go to heaven?"

Do you know how they reply to me? I know you may not believe this; I still have a hard time believing it, but each year they say, "Well, Father, we will go to Mass when we want to and have nothing else to do for forty-five minutes to an hour, depending on who the priest is, and we will try to be good people."

Wrong!

Do you mean to tell me that God is a fool? To make money, to be good in sports, to be a good golfer, to be good at anything, you have to put in hour after hour after hour every day. You have to work really hard, and then you could lose it anyway, even if you get to the top of your game. But, to go to heaven, the greatest of all gifts, the eternity of eternities, all some may think they need to say is, "I will try to be a good person, and I will go to church once in a while." Do you really think that God is a fool? Let me give you a hint—God is not the children's character Barney. He does not sing, "I love you, you love me." We believe that we are saved by grace, but we need to receive this grace and live this grace in order to use our God-given talents if we are to be great in anything on earth. Would you rather be great on earth only or great in God's eyes?

Have you ever thought about what eternity is? Here is something to help you grasp a little bit of what eternity will be like. If you live to be one hundred years old, your time on earth would be equivalent to taking the smallest part of an atom and reducing it by a billion. It's not much time at all, just a blink of an eye!

But eternity can be compared to when a man goes to the beach at Lake Erie, bends down, takes one grain of sand, one tiny, itty-bitty grain of sand, and he slowly takes one step. It takes him ten thousand years to take one step and another ten thousand years to go take another step. This man starts slowly walking and it takes him a billion years to get to the top of Mount Everest. When he gets to the top of Mount Everest, he drops that one grain of sand and slowly, at ten thousand years a step, walks back to the lake. It takes billions of years to get back to Lake Erie and, there, he starts the process again. When this man has taken every grain of sand from every single place on the earth— the bottom of all the lakes, the bottom of the oceans, the bottom of all the little streams—and he slowly takes them to the top of Mount Everest, ten thousand years a step, and puts them on the top of the mountain, and slowly walks back, and when he has every grain of sand at the top of Mount Everest, then eternity is just beginning. It's just beginning. Yet, what we do in this little time on earth determines where our eternity will be. Our time on earth is nothing, yet eternity is everything.

As a young seminarian in college I spent a summer in the Grand Canyon, where I did Ecumenical Ministry. During my time there, every day I would go out and spend my prayer time in the desert. It was kind of interesting. I often felt like Jesus when He was being tempted in the desert, and I thought, Oh, I wouldn't like this for forty days and forty nights.

One morning, I remember talking to God, and I just started to cry. I said, "Lord, when I die and stand before You, I just want to hear You say, 'Well done, good and faithful servant.'" The One I want to please more than anyone else before taking my last breath is the God of the universe. I don't care if the rest of the world thinks that Father Larry was great or awful or if the rest of the world even cares. The only thing I want is for the God of the universe to say, "You did what I wanted you to do." That is why every day, weak as I am, I try to keep that end goal in mind. I want to do only what pleases Him! I live for the day when I will take my last breath and stand before God in judgment, hopefully hearing Him say, "Well done, good and faithful servant."

What do you want? What do you want the God of the universe to say to you when you stand before Him on Judgment Day? You are going to stand before Him one day, too. What are you going to say? Are you living in such a way now that someday He'll say, "Well done"?

As I am writing this, a good friend of mine is dying. She called me and asked me to conduct her funeral Mass; I said, "Oh, you are not dead yet. Stop. Relax." And she said, "I want to make sure before I die that I am at peace with everybody." She has been, actually, writing letters and calling people, in order to reconcile any actual or perceived differences. She is making peace.

If today was your last day on earth, are you at peace with everybody in your life? Are you at peace with everybody in your family? At work? Is there someone you have not yet forgiven? You may have to work on this. It says in the Gospel of Matthew, "If you forgive men their trespasses, your heavenly Father also will forgive you; but if you do not forgive men their trespasses, neither will your Father forgive your trespasses" (6:14–15).

Have you done your best with your talents? Remember the parable of the talents in chapter 25 of the Gospel of Matthew? Jesus tells us about a property owner who was leaving for a journey who called his servants, entrusting them with his property. To one man he gave five talents, to another he gave two, to another he gave one. When he came back, the one who was given five said, "You delivered to me five talents; here I have made five talents more" (Mt 25:20). The property owner replied, "Well done, good and faithful servant" (Mt 25:21). The one who had two talents then said, "You delivered to me two talents; here I have made two talents more" (Mt 25:22). Again, the property owner replied, "Well done, good and faithful servant" (Mt 25:23). Finally, the one that had one talent stood before the property owner and said that he had hidden the one talent that he had, explaining, "I knew you to be a hard man, . . . so I was afraid, and I went and hid your talent in the ground. Here you have what is yours" (Mt 25:24–25). The property owner replied, "You wicked and slothful servant!" (Mt 25:26).

Have you multiplied the talents that God has given you? Have you used them for His glory or your own glory? Have you used the gifts of the God of the universe for Him? Have you multiplied those gifts or have you buried them? If you haven't been using your talents well, it's time! Life isn't over yet. Make a decision that not one of your gifts will be wasted. Use them and multiply them, because that is what's important. Have you been a man of love? Love is a talent. Do your wife and children know you love them? Do you tell them? When they look in your eyes, what do they see? Do they see a man of love? As St. John of the Cross said, in the end, "we will be judged by love alone."

When I was a young boy, my grandmother gave me a medal. The front of the medal had an image of St. Francis Xavier; the back, the words of Jesus that St. Ignatius told St. Francis. St. Francis Xavier was a very gifted man. But as a young man he was worldly—until he met St. Ignatius, who was older. St. Ignatius would constantly challenge St. Francis. St. Ignatius told St. Francis the same thing Jesus Christ said to His apostles in Mark 8:36, the same thing that was on the back of my medal: "What does it profit a man to gain the whole world and forfeit his soul?"

My grandmother gave me that medal when I was in the second grade and it has influenced me ever since. That's why, at seventeen, I couldn't avoid the question "What if I gain everything and I go to hell? What if I gain the whole world and yet I lose the only thing that would make a difference? What if I become a multi-multi-millionaire and everyone thinks I am great, and then when I am lying on my death-bed, I realize that it was all a waste? I wasted it on me. I wasn't a man of love. What if I lose my soul?" Think about it. That is where you have to make a decision. Are you going to live for eternity or are you going to live for today?

By God's grace, I have been ordained a priest for more than twenty years. I have dealt with a lot of people as they were dying. Some people are very afraid. Fear of death is the number one fear. Hebrews 2:14 tells us, "Since therefore the children share in flesh and blood, he himself [Jesus] likewise partook of the same nature, that through death he might destroy him who has the power of death, that is, the devil." Then, it continues with the phenomenal verse that puts everybody in their places. It says, "And deliver all those who through fear of death were subject to lifelong bondage" (Heb 2:15).

Fear of death makes us slaves. You can either decide to spend your life in slavery or spend your life in freedom. You need to make a decision to answer the questions "Where am I concerning the God question? What am I doing about it?" What I am encouraging you to do—before you go on in this book—is if you don't in your heart of hearts know God, to make the commitment of time. You need to say,

"Okay, I am going to spend this much time every day for the next six months getting to know God." It is going to take time. The rest of the book isn't going to make any sense, unless you decide that this is the most important thing you are going to do.

If you want to be a man, then be a man of God. If you want to be a man, then you have to say, "It is going to take me time just like it takes me time to make money, time to be healthy, time to watch sports, time to do all these things. If it takes time to grow in those things, then it is going to take time to get to know God." God must become the most important thing in your life. Money isn't going to keep you alive forever. Being healthy isn't going to keep you alive forever. Sports aren't going to keep you alive forever.

Let me give you a hint: nothing will keep you alive forever except for God. The most important thing you will ever do is seek God. When you come to know Him, He will teach you how to be a man.

Three Tasks You Must Accomplish

1. Be a man who lives with your end in mind. Write down what you want God and others to say about you when you die. These should be your new goals in life. Now set up a plan on what you need to do to reach these goals. Be practical!

2. Be a man who knows God. If you do not know God yet, then decide today that you are going to go and do whatever it takes to get to know Him. Don't wait; life is short, and eternity is forever!

3. Be a man of prayer. Commit yourself to spending at least five minutes a day with God in prayer for the rest of your life, beginning today.

Questions for Reflection and Discussion

1. Do you live for today or for eternity? Explain.

2. What would a person who was honest say about you if you died today? What do you want them to say?

3. Read Matthew 25:31–46. What does Jesus say will happen when He "comes in his glory"? If this were to happen today, which side would you be standing on?

CHAPTER 2

Be a Man Who Lives
as a Beloved Son

You are my beloved Son; with you I am well pleased.
—Mark 1:11

When we want to know what it means to "be a man" we need to look at the ultimate alpha man—Jesus Christ. Jesus became a man to save us and to show us what true manhood is. As we reflect on His life, death, and Resurrection we are confronted with the truth that Jesus was a man for others and that we need to do the same.

Where did Jesus get His strength in His humanity? To answer this question we need to look into His public ministry. His whole ministry began at His baptism. This is so important for us. Always keep in mind that what happens to Jesus needs to happen also to us, and, yes, that includes His crucifixion!

When Jesus Christ was baptized, the sky opened up and the Spirit descended upon Jesus; God the Father spoke and said, "You are my beloved Son" (Mk 1:11). This is where Jesus Christ in His humanity gets His strength to enter into the desert—knowing He is God's Son and receiving the Holy Spirit. After this experience He spent forty days and forty nights in the desert, dwelling on the fact that He was the beloved Son of the Father and dealing with the tempter who tried to sidetrack Him of this fact.

I believe that Jesus had to grow in His knowledge of Who He was, and He willed to do this so He could be like us in *all* things—though there is much debate on this point. He had known it since He was a child in the Temple, when, after being lost, He said, "Did you not know that I must be in my Father's house?" (Lk 2:49). He had the sense of it, but with the baptism when the sky opened up and He heard, "You are my beloved Son", everything changed. Just as Jesus learned He was beloved of the Father, so it must be with us. Where it began with Jesus Christ, it must begin with us.

There are a lot of men's books out now that discuss the "father wound". Every man has a father wound. We are told that we have to deal with our father wounds before we can do anything else. Yes, I buy into it, and, yes, I have a father wound, too. Everybody has a father wound. Okay? Get over it. We can't spend the rest of our lives thinking, "Well, I am the way I am because of my father. He didn't love me the way he should have. He didn't appreciate me enough. He didn't support me enough. He didn't do this, this, and this." Enough already! Time to be a man and move on—again I will help you—read on.

People come to me all the time when I am doing missions and say, "Father, I come from a dysfunctional family." Really? Well, join the crowd. Everybody comes from a dysfunctional family. Let me give you a hint, gentlemen. One day I or another priest will be dealing with your kids, and they are going to say, "Father, I come from a dysfunctional family." Yes, your kids will be saying that about you one day. Why? Because none of us is perfect; there were only two perfect people—Jesus and His Mother, Mary, and we are not either of them! Everybody comes from some type of dysfunctional family. It is our job to deal with it and get over it. We can't let our wounds be something that keeps bringing us down. You need to decide to stop living in the past and using your past as an excuse for your particular dysfunction; you need to deal with your past and then start looking to a future full of hope. "For I know the plans I have for you, says the LORD, plans for welfare and not for evil, to give you a future and a hope" (Jer 29:11). Do not let your past dictate your future!

Christ, of course, never had this Father wound because Christ had a perfect Father. Also, Christ had the best human father and role model in the person of St. Joseph. St. Joseph was a righteous man. Jesus did not go around with a gaping wound inside of Him. We, however, are not perfect, and we do have wounds. The reality is, the only way to heal our father wounds is by letting God the Father be our Father.

We need to know who our true Father is. When Jesus Christ said, "Call no man your father" (Mt 23:9), He did not mean priests. Sometimes people go crazy over this by saying, "Oh, if you are a priest I won't dare call you father because the Word of God says, 'Call no man father.'" However, that has nothing to do with it. They did not even call priests at that time "father". When Jesus uses this term, He's not saying that you should not call any person on earth your father; what He meant was, you should not call the person who begot you, your true father. There's only one Father for everybody: God the Father! That guy you call your dad, he's the instrument of fatherhood, but he's not your true Father.

When we talk about our fathers—whether we had a good father, a bad father, a close and supportive father, or a distant and unsupportive father whom we did not know at all—it doesn't matter as much because the reality is, we all have the same Father in heaven. It's that Father Who will bring healing to us.

The problem is, most of us have never gotten to know our true Father. We have never heard God the Father look at us and say, "You are My beloved son." We have never cherished that truth. Most men go to God out of fear or in an attempt to be a good person. They live their lives in a similar manner as the Pharisees did. Living this way makes us people who just keep the rules instead of people who do everything for the love of our Father.

When I went to the seminary at the age of seventeen, I went because I was afraid of dying. When I came to that experience, however, I came to know that God was real. It was then that I said, "Whatever You want, God, I will do." Still, even then, I didn't know that He loved me. I only knew He existed—God the Father existed. I thought, "Okay, if I do what God wants, then He is going to keep me around. If I don't do what He wants, then He is going to get rid of me, right?" I had the mentality of a high school kid thinking, "Okay, so God is alive and I want to live forever, so I will obey Him." I only went to seminary and tried to obey God because I was afraid of going to hell. That was enough in the beginning, but it wasn't enough for the rest of my life. I thought if I went before God and I was celibate (being a seventeen-year-old virgin even back then was a big deal), then He would accept me. I was still worried, however, because being around Larry, even Father Larry, for more than an hour is too much for some people. I thought that even God the Father, after a couple thousand years of being with Larry, would say, "Okay, that's enough of him", and then He would get rid of me. BAM! After all, He only has to say, "Okay, I don't want you to exist anymore." By the time you respond, "You can't say . . .", you'd be gone. God is God.

I knew I had to please God, but I wasn't trying to please Him for His sake, but for my own. I liked existing. The problem is, if the only reason we come to God and follow Him is because of fear of hell, then we are missing the point. Then who are we really loving? Ourselves! The idea that I only do what I do because I don't want you to get mad at me is inherently selfish.

When I entered seminary, I realized that God was real. I tried to be a good seminarian by doing all the right things and staying out of trouble. I went through two years of Catholic high school seminary. I am one of what we call "lifers". After high school, I did another four years of college seminary, then another four years of major seminary. Starting in my second year of major seminary, I decided to go once a month on a twenty-four-hour silent retreat. For anyone who knows me, you can imagine how difficult it was for me to be silent for twenty-four hours. I always made a twenty-four-hour retreat in a place called Poustinia. *Poustinia* is the Russian word for "desert", and it therefore can also mean a small cabin or a spiritual retreat place for solitary meditation and prayer. It is there that you wait for God to speak.

When I was on my silent retreat, I'd get a Bible and sit in a room with a big cross with no corpus on it. The idea was that I had to crucify myself. A director would usually come in and give me passages to read. I would have to spend an hour on each of these passages. They would be short passages. I would normally read one passage once, twice, ten times, twenty times. I had to spend time with the Word of God because the Word of God has the power to transform us, right? There I was, having already been praying for eight years and being in my second year of major seminary, thinking I had my system down. I prayed once a month for twenty-four hours, and when I was in college seminary, I would spend four hours a day in prayer because

I thought I had to get to know God. I was doing my good stuff because I thought doing good things would make God available to me. I was before Him in His presence.

At the time, my spiritual director was a nun named Sister Joan Wagner. During one of my twenty-four-hour retreats, Sister Joan came in to find me quite excited about spending my twenty-four hours alone with the Lord. We had the following conversation.

"Larry?" she said in the gentle way that nuns address you.

"Yes, Sister?"

"What do you need from God?" she asked me.

"Oh, nothing, Sister. I'm quite happy. Thank you very much", I said.

She looked at me and again said, "Larry?"

"Yes, Sister?"

"What do you need from God?"

"Oh, nothing, Sister. I'm quite happy. Thank you very much, Sister", I replied. However, she was a persistent nun, and I am sure you have met those types.

"Larry?"

"Yes, Sister?"

"What do you need from God?"

Finally, I said, "Joan, I don't know what I need from God. What are you asking me this for?" Nuns are very patient people, so she stood there until I finally added, "Okay, Joan, I guess what I need from God is to be more gentle with people." (Most people know my nickname in seminary was "proud, arrogant, and aggressive Richards". Can you imagine? I think I am so gentle, kind, and loving.)

"Okay, Larry, I want you to spend one hour with Isaiah, chapter forty-three, verses one through five."

At the time, I responded, "Oh, Joan, give me another one; I use that one all the time! That was the way I would end personal letters to people; I would end with verse four of that passage and write, 'You are precious in His eyes; you are honored and He loves you', and then I would add in parentheses 'and so do I! Larry'." She just looked at me and said, "Shut up and let God say that to you for a change!"

"Yes, Joan!" (You can't win when you argue with a nun!)

After she left I began to spend time with God by meditating on the verses. As I said, in Isaiah 43:4 God says, "You are precious in My eyes, you are honored, and I love you."

So, though I was not very excited about spending time with this passage, I thought about the Scripture that says, "To obey is better than sacrifice" (1 Sam 15:22). I then sat on the floor next to my bed and started reading the verse once, twice, three times, four times, five times, ten times, fifty times. I kept reading the same five verses over and over again, and as I was coming to the end of my time, the Holy Spirit started to move from my hard head into my harder heart and started to make me feel uncomfortable. Here is the passage: "But now, thus says the LORD, who created you . . . and formed you . . . : Fear not, for I have redeemed you" (Is 43:1 [RNAB]). Most people live in fear. People fear what is going to happen tomorrow. They fear if they will have enough money. People fear death. Fear. Fear. Fear. We let fear control our lives. However, depending on what translation you have of the Bible, God tells us 365 times in His Word, "Do not Be Afraid."

I've often thought about having a calendar that daily lists a verse that contains the saying "Do not be afraid." People need to be reminded not to live in fear. Every day, God looks at us and says, "I don't want you to be afraid."

Why shouldn't we be afraid? God tells us we should not be afraid because He has redeemed us. He has called you by name. When was the last time you went to pray and you heard God say your name? Probably never? The problem is we're not listening. Think about it. If the Pope were giving a speech in Rome in front of a crowd of a million people and in the middle of his speech he looks at you and calls you by name, what would you do? You would probably look around confused. But he says again, "Yeah, you, Joe. Come here! Come over here!" Then he sends his Swiss Guards to get you. They bring you up and they put you right up next to the Pope, who, in turn, puts his arm around you and says, "Hey, world. I want you to meet my friend Joe. Joe, this is the world." For the rest of your life you would be going around saying, "You know, the Pope called me out of a million people. He knew my name and he showed me to the world." People would talk about you as the person the Pope singled out. You would probably gloat a little too. So what? The Pope knows your name. The God of the universe, the One Who created all things, also knows your name. He calls you by name every day in prayer. We only need to hear Him. God says, "I have called you by name; you are Mine." Think about that. God calls you by name, and you belong to Him. He tells us, "When you pass through the water, I will be with you; in the rivers you shall not drown. When you walk through fire, you shall not be burned; the flames shall not consume you. For I am the LORD, your God, the Holy One of Israel, your savior. I give Egypt as your ransom, Ethiopia and Seba in return for you. Because ..." (Is 43:2–4 [RNAB]). I think the rest of this line is the reason Sister Joan had me sit there for an hour with such a small piece of text. She wanted me to understand what God meant when He said, "Because you are precious in my eyes" (Is 43:4). Try to tell another guy he is precious and let me know how that works out for you. But God the Father looks at you and looks at me and says, "Because you are precious in my eyes and glorious, and because I love you" (ibid.). We must enter into a relationship with God knowing that truth. We must know that our relationship begins where Jesus began, with the knowledge that we are loved by the Father. The God of the universe looks at you and says: "I love you!" Let Him!

As I'm reading this over and over again, I am reminded of what I thought when I was getting my degree in counseling. I've always believed that the deepest need in everyone's heart is to be simply loved. I don't care how tough you are, how self-made you are, or if you are the Pope or the president, you need, everyone needs, to be loved. Until we get that basic need filled, we try to fill that need with other things. Mother Teresa used to say that the people in India would be so hungry that they'd actually go around and pick up dog dung and eat it to try to fill up the emptiness. Likewise, so many men are so unaware of being loved that they take all kinds of dung and eat it to try to fill up the emptiness. Until we know that we are loved, we are going to try to fill up the emptiness with all sorts of things that God doesn't want. That is why He looks at us and says, "You are precious ... and glorious, and ... I love you."

As I was sitting on the floor reading the passage again and again, I started telling God all the reasons why He couldn't love a jerk like me. I was reminded of a certain confession with my spiritual director, who is the exorcist of the Diocese of Erie. I'll never forget going to confession and being aware of my sinfulness. I was on retreat in college seminary out in the woods and confessing my sins to my spiritual director and God. It was the first time I met my spiritual director, so as we were walking to the lodge for confession, he put his arm around me and asked, "What is your name?"

"It's Larry, Father."

Then he looked at me and asked, "Larry, do you know how much God loves you?"

"Oh, yes, Father."

Then all of a sudden I felt a *WHACK!* He hit me in the back of the head and said, "Liar!" and I thought, this guy just hit me and I am going to go to confession to him! I got real nervous. But I knew he was right. I knew in my head that I was loved by the Father; I read the Bible. I just didn't know in my heart that God loved me. If I asked you if you know God loves you, would you lie too? You may know it in your head, but do you know it in your heart?

When Sister Joan had me read the same Scripture passage over and over again, the truth was that I still did not know it in my heart of hearts that God loved me. Though I know that the deepest need is to be loved, at the same time, I was having trouble getting over my own self-hatred. There are things about all of us we don't like or even hate about ourselves. We compare ourselves to others. I'm not as athletic as this one. I'm not as smart as this one. I don't have as good a job. For whatever reason, there is that self-hatred side of every human being. Not just men. That is why we are competitive. The more competitive we are, the more it is okay that I'm not this way or that way because at least I am better than you. The problem with that way of thinking is that there is always somebody better than you eventually. You might be king of the hill today, but everybody wants to get to be king of the hill. They are going to knock you down. Just a thought.

So here it is. Instead of trying to fill up our emptiness inside superficially, we need to accept when God the Creator of the universe looks at you and me and says, "I love you, and you are My son!" When Sister Joan gave me the passage, I tried to tell God all the reasons why He couldn't love a jerk like me. I'm proud. I'm arrogant. I want things done my own way. I have impure thoughts every day of my life. Some people just sit there and think, "Oh, priests never have sexual thoughts." If only! It is part of something I have to struggle with the same way you do. It's only by the grace of God that I have been pure throughout the years. The only way!

So I was telling God all the reasons He could not love me, and, in the midst of this, my spiritual life began. I was sitting there crying out to the God of the universe. I should mention that my image of God was that of my grandmother. As it was, in my prayer, I had this image of my grandmother, and no matter how much I was screaming at God, He just kept repeating, "You are precious in my eyes and glorious." As I continued telling Him all the reasons why He couldn't love me, God began crying like my grandmother used to cry. I remember looking at Him and saying, "God, what are You crying for?" God looked at me and said, "Larry, you hurt Me when you do not allow Me to love you."

Larry, you hurt Me when you do not allow Me to love you.

I call this experience the beginning of my spiritual life because I heard deep within me, clearer than I ever heard anything else in my life, "Larry"—He said my name— "you are My son. In Jesus, you are My son."

"Yes, Father," I said, "I am Your son." Every dam in my life burst open. In my mind I saw my grandmother crying. Then I saw God crying. I was on the floor holding my Bible, crying like a baby because the God of the universe looked at me and said, "In Jesus, Larry, you are My son."

That night I even looked at God and said, "Even speak to me tonight in my dreams." You should not ask God to speak to you in your dreams unless you are ready for what can happen. That night I had a dream and it was a weird dream. I dreamt I was home in Pittsburgh and all my friends and relatives were possessed—Linda Blair possessed: green throw-up, head spinning around, etc. At the time, I wasn't even a priest yet, but, in my dream, what did I do? I started exorcising the demons by saying, "In Jesus' name, leave that person." Nothing! I tried again: "In Jesus' name, leave that person." Nothing! The devil laughed at me, and, you should know, I can't stand being laughed at. I started screaming at the devil, but nothing happened. Then, inside of my dream, the devil started to possess me. (I have told this story a thousand times, and I still get goose bumps from repeating it because I'll never forget how the devil started to possess me.) I then looked down at my hand and his hand popped out of my hand. As I'm saying, "You can't do this to me", my arms started twirling around in a circle and my knees rose up to my chest. I started levitating toward the ceiling. I continued screaming, "You can't do this to me. In Jesus' name . . ." Nothing happened. Then all of the sudden I heard in my dream the same thing I heard in my prayer that night: "Larry, he can't do this to you. In Jesus, you are My son." And as soon as I said, "Yes, Father, I am Your son", the devil screamed and left me. After this experience, I went around to all of my friends and relatives and touched them and said, "You are God's beloved daughter. You are God's beloved son."

When I woke up, I was soaking wet from sweat because the dream felt so real. The next day, Sister Joan asked me, "Well, Larry, did God say anything to you last night?" I told her the story I just told you. She looked at me and said, "Larry, your whole point in ministry will be to tell people who they are—that they are sons and daughters of the Father."

You need to know who you are. Until you know in your heart that you are a beloved son of God, you are just going through the motions. The only way you are going to come to know your true identity is to be silent long enough so that God can tell you. Listen to Him. The main way God speaks to us, gentlemen, is through His Word. We have to spend time with His Word. I had spent time with His Word for years and, like my dream at first, nothing happened. I know now that it was because I read it like a history book. I read it because I had to do something. However, when Sister told me, "I want you to spend an hour with five Scripture verses and let it echo into your being, let God say this to you. Shut up and let God speak to you for an hour", things began to change. Fifty minutes into that hour, God finally got through to my hard head and started touching my harder heart. You and I have to make sure that if we are going to be sons of the Father, we will spend time with His Word. We need to patiently wait until God reveals Who He is and tells us who we are. He told Jesus.

St. Augustine said the best way to communicate with God is through the Psalms. Psalm 2:7 says, "I will tell of the decree of the LORD: He said to me, 'You are my son, today I have begotten you.'"

Please don't try to read the Word of God like you are reading anything else. Don't let it be another book. Some men are so proud about reading the Bible from cover to cover, but did it change their lives? Did they let it enter their being? The Word of God is so powerful, it has the power to reach into your heart and change it. It has the power to change your life. The way I tell people to read the Word of God is first to pray the following prayer to the Holy Spirit: "Spirit of the Living God, speak to my heart your Word." The only one who can speak the Word of

God, and is the Breath of God, is the Holy Spirit. You
need to give the Holy Spirit permission to enter into your
being. Then slowly start reading the Scripture again and
again. Or when you are reading it, read it slowly until God
takes His two-by-four and bashes you over the head like he
did to me when he said, "You are My son. You get that,
Richards?" "Yes, loud and clear, God."

It was a life-changing moment. I had already been praying for six years, an hour minimum per day, but I didn't get
it until God sat there and hit me over the head and said,
"Now get what this is about, Larry. It's not about you. It is
about Who I am to you. I am your Father. You are My
son. Now, would you act like it? Would you act like My
son? Would you be My son in reality? Don't just talk about
'Well, I am a Christian. Nice. Or this is who I am, a Catholic. Nice.'"

Spend time meditating about the baptism of Jesus. Mark
1:11 says, "And a voice came from heaven, 'You are my
beloved Son; with you I am well pleased.'" Likewise in
Luke 3:22 it is written, "And the Holy Spirit descended
upon him in bodily form, as a dove, and a voice came from
heaven, 'You are my beloved Son; with you I am well
pleased.'" In Jesus you are a beloved son of the Father.
Stop reading for a moment and let God, Who is with you
at this very moment, speak to your heart by hearing Him
say, "You are My beloved son, you are My beloved son,
you are My beloved son!" Be still with Him here.

Did you hear Him? Be patient. He will speak these words
to you, but you will need to spend time with Him.

On one of my radio programs I said, "We are adopted
by God." Afterward, a woman wrote in an e-mail, "Father,
that doesn't help."

I responded, "What do you mean, it doesn't help?"

"Well, we should be sons and daughters of the Father just because of the matter of creation."

The thing is, mere creation doesn't make you a son or daughter of the Father. That makes you a creature of God. God is your creator. That's why when this hogwash goes around and we hear, "Oh, don't call God 'Father'; call Him 'Creator'", that's garbage! The reason it is garbage for Christians is it takes out the relationship aspect. If I create a car, I'm the creator of the car, but I don't have a relationship with the car. If God is just our creator, it's not enough. So what? He also created my dog, Rudy, but my dog is not a son of the Father. Rudy is a creature of the Creator. Big difference. When we start playing these games with God and say, "God, you are the creator of all things", we are missing the point. We never enter into a relationship with God. The way that we know who we are is through the sacrament of baptism. The teaching of the Church is clear. The day you and I got baptized, we were adopted by God. When we were baptized, the sky opened up just like it did upon Jesus, and spiritually, God the Father, the Creator of the universe, looked at you and me and said, "You are My beloved son." Whether you got baptized at one month old or whether you were fifty, God looked at you and said, "You are My beloved son." You stopped being a creation of the Father and you became a son of the Father by the power of the Holy Spirit.

Romans 8:15 says, "You did not receive the spirit of slavery to fall back into fear." When we are a slave to anything, it's because of fear. Paul says, "Because you are sons, God has sent the Spirit of his Son into our hearts, crying, 'Abba! Father!' So through God you are no longer a slave but a son" (Gal 4:6–7). God wants to have intimacy with you and with me. Intimacy! Do you know what the word "intimacy" means? Into-me-see. God not only wants to have intimacy looking inside of you, but He wants you to look inside of Him and see Who He is. He's your Father. But He's more than your Father. He's your dad. He's your papa. He's Abba, the Hebrew term used by Jesus that means "Father". To understand the significance of the simple name "Abba" you must understand that in Jewish culture you weren't even allowed to pronounce God's name, Yahweh. If you needed to write it, you had to remove the vowels because you weren't worthy of the name. When the Jewish read the Scriptures, they would simply say, "The Lord. The Lord. The Lord." But both Christ and St. Paul said that when we pray, we should say "Abba" (see Lk 11:2 and Gal 4:6). It's not something you decide to do. It's something that the Spirit of the Living God, which was given to you the day you were baptized, cries out to you for you to do.

There is a difference between you praying and the Spirit of God praying within you. When we are praying we may think, "Did I say this right? I have to say these prayers." A lot of people get into the habit of saying the same prayers over and over again. However, if you just pray the same rehearsed prayers over and over again it can become superstition. We are trying to make God jump through our hoops. "This is what I want, God." "Or, if I want this from God, I had better learn how to say it right." Or, "If I say those ten things they have in the pews, this prayer won't fail." We are trying to manipulate God. Manipulation is not the same as having a relationship. God wants intimacy. Gentlemen, when was the last time during prayer to the Father that you cried out, "Abba. Daddy. Papa"? That is the first part of prayer.

Prayer begins with God's Spirit inside of us. God's Spirit takes control of our prayer and we enter into a relationship.

The Father loves the Son, the Son loves the Father, and their love is so real it's the Spirit. The Spirit's job is to pick us up and to draw us into a relationship with the Trinity. When we cry out "Abba", we enter into intimacy with the Father. The Father then holds us and says, "You are My son."

Spend time with that one word, "Abba", by repeating it. My life gets quite crazy sometimes. One day, for example, I had two funerals. Later, I had prayer time with the area Protestant pastors, and then I had to have a meeting. In the craziness of life, I have found that I need a word to put me into the presence of God. I can go back to my holy hour this morning or my holy hour in the middle of the night. I need something to remind me of the presence of God. For me that word has always been "Abba". When I am getting ready to get upset about something, I remember the word "Abba". I instantly come into the presence of our Father. Instantly! That is the way God can control me instead of me trying to control God.

Gentlemen, I just want to offer this truth to you. Somewhere you have to find who your dad is. Don't try to find him intellectually; find him in your heart. A good way is to surrender to the Spirit and to focus on the word that Jesus said, "Abba." The Spirit comes within us and cries out, "Abba." Jesus, when He taught us to pray, said, "Our Father." Abba. Enter into that reality.

First John 3:1 says, "See what love the Father has given us, that we should be called children of God; and so we are." If I ask you what you are, sometimes you say, "I am a sinner." Okay, we all know that. But what makes us any different than other pagans in the world? We are loved sinners who are sons of the Father. The second part of the foregoing verse and verse 2 continue the thought: "The

reason why the world does not know us is that it did not
know him [Christ]. Beloved, we are God's children now; it
does not yet appear what we shall be, but we know that
when he appears we shall be like him, for we shall see him
as he is." We will find out what is going to happen later
when we see the beatific vision of God. But, we don't have
to focus on that. Now we are God's sons.

A lot of people never understand that our lives are about
relationship. Sometimes it becomes just a ritual. Ritual without relationship is hypocrisy. If we just go through the ritual of praying, we act like the Pharisees. They said all their
prayers, but without heartfelt meaning. Ritual without intimacy is not God's plan. Pray in the arms of God.

We need to know how blessed we are! Do you know
that only 32 percent of the world is Christian? Only 32
percent. That means that of all the people in the world,
only 32 out of 100 people even have the knowledge that
God is our Father. In Islam, God is the Great Other. He is
all merciful. He is all good. But God is never Father. Christ
came to reveal to us that God is our Father. We need to
really spend time with one of the most unique revelations
of God, through Jesus Christ, that He is my dad and I'm
His son. If any of you are fathers, you would never let anyone hurt your son without going through you first. Remember, when God the Father in the Old Testament says, "You
are the apple of My eye" (see Zech 2:8, Deut 32:10), He is
really saying, "I can't do anything without looking at you."
Do you ever think about this reality? There is never one
moment when God is not thinking about you. Not one
moment!

God is always thinking about you. He's always with you.
A like comparison is our breathing. If we stop breathing,
we die. Yet how often, though it is the core of our lives

and it keeps us alive, do we think about breathing? The same is true with the Fatherhood of God. It's God's love that keeps us alive. But how often do we dwell on that? Do we spend time with that? Paul tells us when we spend time with our Father, "You are no longer a slave but a son" (Gal 4:7). You will no longer be afraid; you will be a son. You will no longer be hurt. God will show you what a real Father is. Before we can think about what we have to do, we have to think about who we truly are. Then, only once we accept who we are, do we figure out what we have to do. Because I am God's son, because I have God's Spirit within me, this is the way I will live my life. I don't live my life in such a way to become God's son. I am God's son. What we shall later be has not yet come to life. It begins with a Father and a son—you and God!

Three Tasks You Must Accomplish

1. Be a man who lives as a beloved son. Be still and let God embrace you as His son. As He spoke to Jesus, let Him speak to you: "You are my beloved son." After spending time in His embrace, respond to Him and take five minutes to pray the "Our Father" from the depth of your being to your Father who is with you.

2. Be a man who reads the Bible. Decide to spend time reading Scripture every day, for it is here that God will speak to you and reveal His will to you. Live "No Bible, no breakfast; no Bible, no bed!"

3. Be a man who listens more than he talks. This begins with your relationship with God. Never leave your prayer time without giving time to silence.

Questions and Actions for Reflection and Discussion

1. Do you really know who you are in the heart of your Father God? Explain.
2. What do you think that you have to do specifically to grow in relationship with your heavenly Father?
3. What are the obstacles that keep you from committed time with God, and how are you going to overcome them?

CHAPTER 3

Be a Man Who Repents

The time is fulfilled, and the kingdom of God is at hand; repent, and believe in the gospel.

—Mark 1:15

After praying in the Holy Spirit and in His humanity alone with His Father for forty days in the desert, the first public words out of Jesus Christ's mouth were a proclamation of John the Baptist. John the Baptist was preparing the way by preaching about repentance. Jesus took up where John the Baptist left off by bringing it into a deeper reality. He doesn't just say repent. He says repent and believe in the Good News. Our lives are not only about turning away from evil, but also about turning toward God. Our lives are about embracing the journey and letting go of the past. We must become new men.

Christ teaches us how to be men through repentance. The problem is nobody likes repentance. Most people today come to Jesus Christ on their own terms: "What are You going to do for me today?" or "If You don't give me what I want then I am mad and I am leaving." Jesus is telling us that we have to change our minds, our attitudes, and our ways of life. Repentance comes from the word "metanoia", which means "to turn". If we are truly going to be disciples of Christ, truly going to be men, we have to stop running away from the reality of the sin in our lives. We have to start dealing with it.

In conversations before hearing confessions, way too often, some people start by making excuses for their sins. "Oh, Father, I am this way because I had a bad family or because I am weak." All these things are true but beside the point. If someone hurts you, you want him to stop and to be sorry—the same with God! We find excuses for our sinfulness, instead of being men and being accountable.

So now let us explore just what sin is. Before we can repent of sin we need first to recognize sin. So, we begin at the beginning in the Book of Genesis. Genesis 3:1 says, "Now the serpent was more subtle than any other wild creature that the Lord God had made."

Who was "the serpent"? The serpent was the devil (Satan or Lucifer). The name "Lucifer" means "light bearer". He was a seraph angel. People often have images of the devil as this ugly being with horns and a pitchfork, but St. Paul tells us that Satan can appear as an "angel of light" (2 Cor 11:14). The devil will usually not appear to you as something ugly. He will appear as an angel of light, as something that seems good or beautiful. This is why it is so important that we as men have a discerning spirit through the Holy Spirit. We have to have a discerning spirit or we will be seduced. We are attracted by beauty. That is why a lot more men than women are caught up in pornography. Men are attracted to the external. We are tempted with our eyes, and the devil knows this, so he appears as an angel of light, as something beautiful.

Next, the devil instills doubt in our hearts by asking questions. In the Book of Genesis, the devil asked the woman, "Did God say, 'You shall not eat of any tree of the garden'?" (Gen 3:1). The woman answered, "We may eat of the fruit of the trees of the garden; but God said, 'You shall not eat of the fruit of the tree which is in the midst of the garden, neither shall you touch it, lest you die'" (Gen 3:2–3).

So the serpent said to the woman, "You will not die" (Gen 3:4).

For God to be a God of love, He needs to give us a choice; He will not make us love Him, so God invites us to either love Him and obey Him or choose to do things our way. So the choice is between death and life.

The devil says you will not die. It is up to Adam and Eve and, ultimately, us to make a decision. Who will we believe? Will we believe God or will we believe Lucifer? God said if you sin, you'll die. Later, in Romans, it says that "the wages of sin is death" (Rom 6:23). As I have said, for us, sin is not that big of a deal. To God it is a very big deal. It cost Jesus His life, and it can cost you your life.

It is as if God says, "Who are you going to believe, Me or Lucifer?" Adam and Eve believed the devil. They believed themselves and the devil because they looked at themselves and they no longer looked at God. They did not trust Him. The serpent says, "You will not die" (Gen 3:4). This is why Jesus called him "the father of lies" (Jn 8:44)! Who are you going to believe?

Now please don't put the original sin on Eve only! Eve gets a bad rap, but where was Adam during the temptation of Eve? He was right next to Eve. Adam was right there with his wife the whole time. The problem was Adam was not being the man God had created him to be. He was to protect his wife but Adam was being a wimp. He kept his mouth shut. He needed to be a true spouse to his wife and say to Satan, "You don't get to my wife except through me." The same thing happens in a lot of marriages today. One of the purposes of marriage is to do everything in your power to get your spouse and family to heaven. A husband is called to be his wife's strength when she is tempted. It can be a sin to keep your mouth shut when the truth in love needs to be spoken.

Marriage is a sacrament of unity. God made you one. However, poor Adam kept his mouth shut, so Eve became fair game. God said they could do anything, except take from the tree of knowledge of good and evil. This is important because it was a test. Like I said before, God has to give us a choice. He will never make any of us stay with Him forever. In the beginning, what God said can be interpreted as, "Listen, you can do anything you want; just don't take from that tree." All sin is a choice between God and that which is not from God, that which is against God's will.

The simplest definition of sin is disobedience to God. What happens, especially for men in America, is we want to make our own rules. But God is God. He gets to make the rules, and He did. It is amazing that fathers do not obey God, especially since they are very adamant about their children obeying them. "You will obey me because I am the father." How nice. God the Father has more of the right to ask of us, even demand of us, that we too obey Him since He created us.

Americans like to vote. Let's be democratic about it. God, however, does not operate a democracy. God is God. If He says something is wrong, and then 99.9 percent of the world votes against it because they believe it is right, it is still wrong. Right? Let's pretend you have ten children and your ten children take a vote one day and they say, "Dad, we don't like the rule you have about us being in bed by nine o'clock. We voted against it. We are going to stay up until midnight." You would not say, "Oh, that is just wonderful.

Please, anything you want." As a father you would whack them and say, "Get to bed at nine o'clock. You do as I say." So here is the God of the universe and He makes the rules, but the devil says not to listen to somebody else.

Years ago on television I saw Tom Cruise being interviewed by Barbara Walters on one of the news shows. It went something like this.

"Tom", addressed Barbara Walters.

"Yes, Barbara", Tom Cruise responded.

"You used to be Catholic, didn't you?"

"I did."

"Well, what happened? You're now what, a Scientologist? Well, can you explain to us why?"

"Of course, Barbara", Tom said. "Do you know Christians, all those Catholics and all those types of people, well you know, they always have to follow somebody else's rules. In Scientology, we make our own."

Tom Cruise thought he was cool, but he was no cooler than Adam and Eve when way back they thought they could become like God. Who is Tom Cruise to determine what is right and wrong? Who are we? A lot of men like to make their own rules because we like to be self-sufficient. If we believe something is right, then it is right. If we believe it is wrong, it is wrong. What are we doing, then? We are trying to take the place of God. We are saying, "I won't listen to anybody else. I am God. I decide." When we usurp the position of God in our lives, we make ourselves God, and we worship our will instead of obeying God. That is not being a man—that is being a coward. That is being prideful. That is a fallacy. We forget that we cannot even take our next breath without God saying, "Okay, I will let you take that next breath." We are totally dependent creatures. Play God all you want, but one day it will be proven that you are not God.

Genesis continues, "The woman saw that the tree was good for food, and that it was a delight to the eyes, and that the tree was to be desired to make one wise" (3:6). All sin has all three of those components. There is something good in it, something desirable, and there is something pleasurable in it. Always, we choose what we *think* is good. We want to do good. When we sin it is because we want it. We are choosing what is an apparent good for us. We have a desire to sin, gentlemen. Be honest with yourself. The Catholic Church teaches that the "tendency to sin", which we all have within us, is called concupiscence. Concupiscence is what we have inside of us—a desire to rebel.

The first thing a lot of sin has is some kind of pleasure in it, some kind of lust. There is a lot of lust to go around— sexual lust, lust of money, lust for possessions. Once you start giving in to lust, just one inch, you usually open the door to give in completely to it, and, the next thing you know, you make a choice and you have to live with the consequence. The very first thing that sin does to us is kill us. Simple. Sin always kills us. God is not a liar!

The second thing sin does is it makes us its slave. Jesus said, "I say to you, every one who commits sin is a slave to sin" (Jn 8:34). If you do not think you are a slave to sin, then try to stop by your own power! You might start to try, innocently enough, but soon you are controlled by your sin—you become a slave.

The third thing that sin does is make you feel dirty. It hurts your soul. It makes you feel guilty inside. Everybody has a conscience; it is gift from God. For example, we know without ever being taught, without ever going to Catechism class, and without ever reading the Bible—even a pagan knows—that it is a bad thing to kill our children.

There is something inside of you that says, "I am going to preserve my kids and not kill them."

The last thing that sin does is separate us from the Father. It is not a punishment. We can imagine God asking, "Who will you believe? Me or Satan? Will you follow Me and want to be with Me or do you want to follow him and do what he wants?" We then choose and then God says, "Okay, I'll give you what you want." God gave us free will. Ultimately, when you drop dead, God will give you what you love the most forever. He'll give you what you want. If what you love is anything other than Him, that is what He will give you. By definition, however, that is hell. Hell is simply separation from God. If you drop dead now, in the midst of reading this book, God will say, "Okay, son, I love you and will give you what you love the most forever." So the question is, what do you love more than anything?

In an attempt to encourage people to attend the nightly parish missions I preach throughout the country, I ask them a very simple question: "Listen; how many of you would be here every night, if I said whoever comes to this parish mission for all four nights will get one million dollars on the last night?" Everyone usually laughs and raises his hand. If I were actually to award the money, people would come from around the world. Why? They love money. Then I ask, "If you would come for a million dollars, why would you not come because you love Jesus?" I know, they hate me, but why would so many people do anything for money but do very little for God?

Many Christians are really using God for their "fire insurance": "I'll go to church on Sunday. I'll do the least I have to do so I won't burn in hell later." A lot of these people would never come to a mission or a retreat, but they will go watch a Notre Dame game—getting there the night before—go to all the pregame activities, drink beer, and have a fine time, and spend two days doing this and not even a blink an eye. Wow. By their actions they show that they love sports more than they love God. God says, "Choose! Do you want to be with Me or don't you? And if you do, prove it." Very simple! Prove it, gentlemen.

Once we know what sin is, we must deal with what Jesus said: "Repent, and believe" (Mk 1:15). Jesus does not just want us to stop our sin; He wants us to stop living our lives "our way" and start living our lives "God's way". Many men love Frank Sinatra's song "I Did It My Way". That is a true guy song. I love that song. *"I stood tall, I did it all, and I did it my way."* You do realize that that is the theme song of those in hell, don't you? God is asking us to live life His way, not our way. Jesus, *the* perfect man, prayed, "Not as I will, but as thou will" (Mt 26:39), to give us an example of how to live as a man!

When Jesus said to repent, He was not only talking to the most obvious of sinners. Jesus, like John before Him, was talking to the Pharisees. The Pharisees were following God their way. They were obeying all the laws, which they thought would make them holy. They thought they were doing it God's way because they followed God's commandments, but they didn't do it for love of God; they did it for love of themselves. They wanted to be holy for themselves. The same is true with us. We should not come to God and follow Him for what He is going to do for us or follow God because we are afraid of hell. The Church always taught that fear of hell is enough to get you to heaven. It's like when your kids do something because they want to or they are afraid of Dad. If they do it because they are just afraid of Dad, then it is not out of love. It is a selfish act. If the only reason we come to Christ and obey Him is because we are afraid of hell, then it is ultimately a selfish reason. I am doing it for me; I am not doing it as an act of love.

When I used to deal with my high school boys, I would have the following conversation:

"Gentlemen, you would never commit adultery on your wife, would you?" I'd ask.

"Never, Father!" they'd answer.

"Why wouldn't you commit adultery against your wife? Is it because the commandment says you shall not commit adultery? Is that why you wouldn't do it?"

"Well, no, Father."

"Then why wouldn't you do it?" I'd ask.

"Because I love her and I wouldn't want to hurt her."

Ding, ding, ding, ding!

Exactly. Until we come to know that it is not just about keeping ourselves out of hell, we will always sin. However, when you love God and decide you do not want to hurt Him because you are in a relationship with Him, then your love for God is what will keep you from sin. We have to pray that we will fall in love with Him more and more each day. It is love that will set you free!

Being sorry is not enough. We need to believe in the Good News. What is the sum of all the Good News? You are loved by God. It will not work just to say, "I'm going to be a man and not sin anymore." No matter how manly you are, you will still fall flat if you try to do it by yourself. Self-control is not enough. Believe in the Good News. You are loved, and you are not in this alone. Jesus said to repent and believe. He invites you into an intimate relationship with God, your Father.

When I conduct men's conferences, during confession I often hear something like: "Father, I have been struggling with the same sin all my life for the last twenty years."

"You don't get it, do you?" I'll say. They always look at me like I'm trying to start a fight, so I say, "Tell me that line again. Give me your excuse again."

"I've always been struggling . . ."

"Stop."

"I've always been . . .", they'll try again.

"Stop."

"I've always . . ."

"Stop."

"I've . . ."

"Stop", I'll say one more time; but this time I'll pose a new question. "What is the problem with what you have been saying?"

They'll lower their heads and think about it for a moment then say, "I."

If you are going to try to deal with your sin yourself, you are going to fail. Let me give you a hint now. Being a Christian is not about being a moral person. Being moral is simply a symptom, but it's not what it's about. As I have said many times, you see moral Muslims. Most Muslim people, not the radical fundamentalists, are extremely moral. They pray many times a day; they fast; they try to be good to everyone. They are extremely moral. Jewish people are extremely moral, too. I bet you even know some atheists that are extremely moral people. Morality does not make you a disciple of Christ. A disciple of Christ is a person who is willing to die to himself and enter into a relationship with Jesus. All relationships require change. When you get married, you give up your life for your wife and you enter into this new relationship. You become one with your wife. When you become a disciple of Christ and repent, it means you give up your old life and you enter into a new life—a relationship of love. Galatians 2:20 says, "I have been crucified with Christ; it is no longer I who live, but Christ who lives in me; and the life I now live in the flesh I live by faith in the Son of God, who loved me and gave himself for me." When you are struggling with sin, you have to get out of your own way and let Christ deal with it. Men hate that. They have to hand over control. We love being in control, don't we? It's my favorite thing. My greatest sin is my favorite thing: wanting to control my own life. Since I am not even in control of my next breath, the whole idea of control is a lie. I have to realize God is in control and hand my life over to Him.

The first step in repentance is allowing the Holy Spirit to convict you of your sin. Now this is not about God condemning you, but showing you what it is in your life that leads you to death and slavery. St. Paul makes it very clear in Romans 8:1: "There is therefore now no condemnation for those who are in Christ Jesus." God does not want to condemn you—He wants to set you free!

He does this most perfectly through the sacrament of confession. When was the last time you went to confession? Well, it is time! Don't be afraid; suck it up and decide you are going to do it—go this week. Almost all of my best encounters with God have come through this wonderful sacrament. It is time to stop making excuses for why you have not gone; God is inviting you home—don't say no.

Now, I want to tell you how to make a good confession. First, pray to the Holy Spirit and ask Him to convict your heart of your sin and ask Him for the grace of repentance. It is only His grace that will open you up to a new beginning. So if you are going to be a man, when you come into a relationship with God, you first have to ask God, "What is wrong in my life? What is it in my life that displeases You?" The Holy Spirit will reveal the answers by convicting you of your sin. The Spirit that has lived inside of you since your baptism will start convicting your heart. You are going to have to give God permission to convict you. Most of us will never ask God about the errors in our lives because we are too afraid to deal with our sins.

If you need help in knowing what sins are holding you in bondage, here is the list that I give to people to help them examine their conscience before confession; it is not an exhaustive list, but it will get you started:

Abortion: helping, paying for a woman to have one
Adultery
All use of illegal drugs
Any dealing with the occult, i.e., Ouija boards
Artificial birth control
Blasphemy: disrespect toward God or toward His Holy Name
Breaking promises deliberately
Bringing dishonor to family, school, community, or the Church
Calumny: telling lies about another
Despair: to believe that God will refuse to forgive you
Destruction of other people's property
Detraction: telling an unkind truth about another
Disobedience toward parents/teachers
Drunkenness, including any drinking under the age of twenty-one
Excessive materialism
Gluttony: eating or drinking to excess
Gossip: talking about others
Hatred
Homosexual actions
Impure thoughts
Indifference to good or evil

Ingratitude

Jealousy

Laziness

Lying

Malice: the deliberate choice of evil

Masturbation: impure actions with yourself

Missing Mass on any Sundays or Holy Days of
Obligation

Murder

Not praying *every* day

Not giving to the poor and the Church

Premarital sex, including oral sex, intercourse, impure
touching of another

Presumption: sinning and saying God *must* forgive you

Pride

Prostitution

Reckless driving that endangers you or your passen-
gers, or others

Rudeness

Selfishness

Stealing

Superstition

Unjustified anger

Using others for your own personal gain

Watching or looking at pornographic material

Now, this list is a good start, but it is important to go deeper
than the symptoms of our sins; instead, we need to go to
the core of our sins. Oftentimes we look at only the external manifestations of our sins. If our sin is lust, we will
look at the symptom—having sex out of wedlock or view-
ing pornography. The real sin, however, is internal—not
trusting God, wanting things our own way, fear of death.

We think, "If I could only deal with this part of my life, I'd be fine." What our symptoms are really showing us is that we have not fully surrendered our lives to God. Instead of saying, "I keep struggling with swearing", you should be saying, "I'm struggling with swearing, but what I have to do is surrender my life to Jesus more." We must come before the Holy Spirit and give Him permission to reveal to us, not only the symptoms of our sins, those things that offend Him, but also our core sins.

The second step to repentance comes after we are convicted of our sins. We, then, must take responsibility for them and then confess them to a priest. Now some people do not believe that you need to confess your sins to a priest, but Sacred Scripture states differently. Jesus gave the power to priests to forgive sins in John 20:22–23 when He said, "Receive the Holy Spirit. If *you* forgive the sins of any, they are forgiven; if *you* retain the sins of any, they are retained" (italics mine). Later, in the Book of James, we read, "Therefore confess your sins to one another" (5:16).

When we do not want to go to confession it is because of our pride, which is really the core of all sin. It is time to humble yourself and swallow your pride, so that you may be healed!

The first thing God wants you to do is stop making excuses for your sin. Take responsibility. Making excuses for our sins is just another way of dismissing the importance of them. My spiritual director would often close my confession by saying, "Isn't it great that God loves a jerk like you?" Absolutely! Honestly, sometimes I choose to sin. Sometimes I like being mad. So do you. We all have our core sins. We play games and make excuses, when we should be men and say, "This is what I have done because I chose to do it. I chose sin. I am sorry, and by God's grace I am going to stop!" Stop the excuses.

Now, when you go to confession you need to have the intention to stop committing the sins. To repent means to make a resolution that you are done with sin. This is our next step. We will always struggle until we come to really repent. I had a great friend who became a Lutheran pastor. We were in seminary at the same time, though two different seminaries. We used to love to talk. We called each other back and forth. We prayed with each other. He is a good, good man of God, although he used to love to say to me, "Larry, do you know what the problem with you Catholics is?"

"What is that, Doug?" I would say.

He'd say, "You Catholics are always confessing, but never repenting." The way he saw it, Catholics kept going to confession, but never changed.

"Oh, Doug, you don't understand the teaching, though. To be forgiven you have to repent or confession does nothing", I would tell him.

We have to have a true repentance. To have a repentant heart means that we decide, when the Spirit of God convicts us and we take responsibility for our sins, that we are done with those sins. In the Catholic Church, when someone prays the Act of Contrition, what does one say after "Oh my God, I am heartily sorry for having offended You . . . and I firmly resolve with the help of Your grace"? "To sin no more." It doesn't say, "I'm going to try to sin no more." It says, by the grace of God, one will sin no more. Until we have that intention in our minds, we are truly not repentant.

A good example is someone who is afraid to fly and who has been in an adulterous relationship against his wife for a year. If right before he gets on the flight, he goes to a priest and says, "Father, I have committed adultery. I'm sorry, Father", but, if in his mind he is thinking, "But, if I survive this flight, I am going back to my mistress", then that confession is not valid. His heart has not decided to stop sinning. He is not forgiven!

Why do we need grace? Let's say you are convicted of your sin, and you take responsibility and then repent. Let's say one of your sins is yelling at your wife. When you confess this sin you must have the intention to stop yelling at your wife. Period.

To illustrate this point let me give you another example. Let's say that I come up to you and I beat you and break your arms, and then a little bit later I come to you and I say that I am sorry and ask you for your forgiveness. Because you are such a saint you say, "Sure, Father, I forgive you!" What a guy you are.

A couple of hours later, I see you again and I say, "Hi, guy." Then I proceed to beat you up again, but this time I break both of your legs. As you are lying on the ground in a bloody mess, I say, "Oh, I am so sorry!"

And then you might even again say, "That is okay, Father; you must have been having a bad day."

I then see you again the next day and I say, "Hi, guy!" and you are a little afraid this time and very cautiously say, "Hi, Father!" Then, this time I punch you in the face and break your nose. Trying to ignore the blood running down your face, I say, "Oh, guy, please forgive me. I am so sorry", and this time I am crying.

What would you say? "Well, that is okay, Father"? No, you would not! You would eventually say to me, "I don't believe you, Father."

Why would you not believe me? Because if I were really sorry I would stop hurting you!

Ding, ding, ding, ding! It is the same thing in our relationship with Almighty God. If I go to confession, I have to then say, "Lord, I am not going to do this sin anymore." The intention has to be there. In our weakness we might still fall, but until the intention is there we'll never really deal with our sins. Trying is not good enough. It is not going to work. You must say, by God's grace, "I won't commit this sin again." That is when you can begin to deal with sin and start to repent.

With confession and repentance there needs be true sorrow. Second Corinthians 7:10 says, "Godly grief produces a repentance that leads to salvation and brings no regret, but worldly grief produces death." What this means is that you should be sorry with Godly sorrow because you hurt your relationship with Him, not that you got caught or because you have to suffer punishment. Let's say you steal a thousand dollars from me and you are afraid I am going to send you to jail. You come to me and say, "Oh, I am so sorry, Father." If I know that the only reason you are sorry is because you think I am going to press charges, I am not going to want to be very merciful. If you come to me, however, and are truly sorry, because you hurt me, I am going to be very merciful.

God is mercy itself, but when we confess we need to have a Godly sorrow. "I'm sorry, Lord, because I have hurt You, Who love me, and I do not want to hurt you." Ray Boltz has a song called "Feel the Nails". The song says, "Does He still feel the nails every time I fail? Does He hear the crowd cry, Crucify, again? Am I causing Him pain? Then I know I've got to change. I just can't bear the thought of hurting Him." The song rings true when we realize that we have to change because we are causing Him pain.

After you confess your sins to a priest, listen to the advice he gives you and then do the recommended penance as soon as possible. This will give you a great new beginning, for when you go to confession, Jesus gives you a new life, sets you free from your slavery, cleanses you of your sins, and reconciles you to our Father!

And once you have been forgiven, make sure that you go to Jesus and thank Him for dying for you and your sins. Because for God to forgive you, Jesus Christ had to die, just so you could live—so live in gratitude!

Once you've apologized to God, you have to decide to do two things. First, you have to pray for strength. That means you go before the Lord and say, "I don't have the power but you do." We as Catholics believe that we are not saved by either faith or works alone; it is faith and works and we do this by God's grace. Grace saves us because we do not have the power to save ourselves. We have to say to God, "God, I'm sorry, but I don't have the power. I have the resolution never to do this again, but I don't have the power. You have to help me." Then, we have to do the second step, which is to get out of the way. St. Paul struggled three times with a painful thorn in his flesh. "Three times I begged the Lord about this, that it should leave me", St. Paul said; but Jesus responded, "My grace is sufficient for you, for my power is made perfect in weakness" (2 Cor 12:8–9). Like St. Paul, we have to accept the power of Christ, through His Holy Spirit.

We are not alone in our battle with Satan. Jesus went to battle with Satan. After He was baptized, Jesus was tempted by Satan, and He defeated him with the Word of God (see Mt 4:1–11; Mk 1:12–13; Lk 4:1–13). Likewise, we need to battle with Satan also, gentlemen.

Traditional Catholic teaching tells us that there are three things we deal with in our struggle with sin: the world, the flesh, and the devil.

The world is just the way people see things, the worldly way of looking at things. It is following the world and its standards instead of following God and doing His will to live our lives. Every time you turn on the TV you are being bombarded with the world and its beliefs.

The struggle with the flesh is with our own needs, our own hungers, and our own wants. It manifests itself in our physical desires and temptations.

The devil can tempt us, oppress us, or, God forbid, possess us. I do not believe that all of our struggles are from the devil, though I firmly believe that he is "like a roaring lion, seeking some one to devour" (1 Pet 5:8). We need to be diligent against him! Saying the prayer to St. Michael every day is an excellent way to defeat his temptations. Here it is:

> Saint Michael the Archangel,
> defend us in battle.
> Be our protection against the wickedness and
> snares of the devil.
> May God rebuke him, we humbly pray;
> and do Thou, O Prince of the Heavenly Host,
> by the Divine Power of God,
> cast into hell Satan and all the evil spirits,
> who roam throughout the world seeking the
> ruin of souls. Amen.

Matthew 4:1 tells us, "Then Jesus was led up by the Spirit into the wilderness to be tempted by the devil." He did this to show us how to be men in the face of temptation, how to be strong in our fight against evil. Jesus fasted and He was hungry. The tempter approached Him and said, "If you are the Son of God, command these stones to become loaves of bread" (Mt 4:3). He tempted Jesus. Jesus replied, "It is written, 'Man shall not live by bread alone, but by every word that proceeds from the mouth of God'" (Mt 4:4).

Jesus shoved God's Holy Word down the throat of Satan and Satan left Him. If Jesus overcame temptation by using the Word of God, He is showing us how to do the same!

Don't run. Don't say, "I am weak." Don't say, "I'm afraid of the devil." We must confront the devil when he is tempting us. We have to take God's Word, which gives us the power, and attack our temptation with it. Invite Jesus Christ, the Word of God, into every temptation. When you are being tempted, the devil will tell you, "Keep it in the dark. Don't bring it to Christ." I always tell men when they are being sexually tempted to say, "Jesus will take care of this for me." Invite Him into the temptation. He is the Word of God, and He is much stronger than Satan. He has already proved it.

Gentlemen, once you have found your core sins, find and memorize the Scripture verses that will help you to confront those sins. When you are being tempted, recall the Scripture and shove it down the devil's throat when he tempts you, and you will be victorious.

In Hebrews it says, "In your struggle against sin you have not yet resisted to the point of shedding your blood" (Heb 12:4). This does not mean that you have not died. It means that you have not given your struggle totally to Christ yet. You have not been crucified with Christ. You have to surrender everything to Him Who will save you. Discipline yourselves, and use the Word of God. Those things will help you become victorious and live a life of repentance. It will help you live this life of repentance instead of believing you are weak. In Christ you are strong. Focus not on yourself and your weaknesses; focus on Christ and His strength.

God is waiting for you. Go to confession, have courage, and be a man who repents.

Three Tasks You Must Accomplish

1. Be a man who repents. Make a good examination of conscience and if you are Catholic make a good confession. No excuses!

2. Be a man who fights against temptation with God's Word. After you have discovered your core sins, look up verses in the Bible and commit them to memory so you can defeat temptations when they arise.

3. Be a man who daily strives to grow in your manhood. Make a nightly examination of conscience and commit yourself to go to confession at least once a month.

Questions and Actions for Reflection and Discussion

1. If you do not go to confession regularly, why not? What are you going to do about it?

2. What are you doing, or what are you going to start doing, to get your family to heaven?

3. How do I prove that I love God above everything? Do I?

CHAPTER 4

Be a Man Who Lives
in the Holy Spirit

Then Jesus was led up by the Spirit into the wilderness.
—Matthew 4:1

Gentlemen, the key to being a man of God is surrender to the Holy Spirit!

Jesus, in His humanity, was always guided by the Holy Spirit. If we want to be true men of God we must embrace our humanity in the same way Jesus did in the Holy Spirit. When I am working with men who are trying to discern God's will, I ask, "Where is the Spirit of God leading you?" Normally they say, "I don't know." They normally do not know because they have never asked!

We should never make any decisions, especially major decisions, without first surrendering to the Spirit of God. If we do not surrender to the Spirit of God, we could often be doing our will instead of God's will. This can get us into trouble. Jesus, Who is God, was led by the Holy Spirit. When a person becomes a Christian, there needs to be a new creation inside of him. Being baptized is not like graduating, where you celebrate a singular event. You can get baptized, even confirmed, and still be a pagan if you do not surrender your life completely to the Spirit of God.

In Genesis we read, "In the beginning, when God created the heavens and the earth, the earth was a formless wasteland, and darkness covered the abyss, while a mighty wind swept over the waters" (1:1–2 [RNAB]). The Hebrew translation of the word "wind" is *ruah*. The word *ruah* is the Hebrew word for wind, spirit, and breath. This wind that was over the chaos was the Holy Spirit. The chaos is there, and what brings this chaos into order is the Spirit of God, the Wind of God.

Next, we see how God makes all creation. In Genesis, He makes man out of dirt, plain old dirt. What gives this dirt life is, again, the Spirit of God communicated through the Breath of the Father. The Scriptures state, "Then the LORD God formed man of dust from the ground, and breathed into his nostrils the breath of life" (Gen 2:7). From the very beginning, it was the Holy Spirit Who gave us life.

An easy way to illustrate the Holy Spirit is to see Him as what tradition sometimes calls Him—the animator. We know what animation is. If you read the Sunday comics, you can see that although the comic communicates something, it is really just static drawings. But, if you watch those comics become cartoons on TV, you see them gain life through animation. The Spirit is our animator. He is the one who gives us life. Inherently, through creation, everybody has some part of God's Spirit or they would not be alive. The very fact that you and I exist shows us that God's Spirit is already working in us. Now God's grace is working in us to try to get us to come into a deeper relationship with God through His Spirit.

Often you hear the phrase "born again". Absolutely, positively, you must be born again. But what does it mean to be born again? Often people will say to be born again means that you accept Jesus Christ as your Lord and Savior. But, that is not what Jesus said "born again" means. John 3:1–3 tells us, "There was a man of the Pharisees, named

Nicodemus, a ruler of the Jews. This man came to Jesus by night and said to him, 'Rabbi, we know that you are a teacher come from God; for no one can do these signs that you do, unless God is with him.' Jesus answered him, 'Truly, truly, I say to you, unless one is born anew, he cannot see the kingdom of God.' " Another translation of the phrase "born anew" is "born again". Nicodemus is surprised and responds, "How can a man be born when he is old? Can he enter a second time into his mother's womb and be born?" (Jn 3:4). Jesus replies, "Truly, truly, I say to you, unless one is born of water and the Spirit, he cannot enter the kingdom of God" (Jn 3:5).

This, of course, means the sacrament of baptism! That is how a person is born again. But the sacrament of baptism is not magic. It gives us the gift of sanctifying grace, but we need to accept this gift! It is like giving someone who is broke and homeless a wrapped box with one million dollars in it and he never opens the gift and starves to death. This is happening to too many people who call themselves Catholic or Christian! You have to open the great gift of the Holy Spirit that is given to you at baptism, and then confirmed in you in the sacrament of confirmation, and cooperate and surrender to God within you! Thus, being born again means surrendering your life fully to the Spirit of the Living God, Who has lived inside of you since your baptism! There needs to be a B.C. and an A.D. in someone's life. Before Christ you were a pagan, but now that the Spirit of God has taken control of your life, you are renewed.

To be a man means that we surrender and let God control our lives. That is almost intuitively opposite of what we want. We love to be in control of our lives. We love it.

In chapter 16 of John, Jesus says, "I tell you the truth: it is to your advantage that I go away, for if I do not go away, the Counselor will not come to you; but if I go, I will send him to you. And when he comes, he will convince the world of sin and of righteousness and of judgment" (Jn 16:7–8). Isn't that amazing? The Spirit is not just this gentle being. The Spirit is going to convict the world of its sin with justice and condemnation. Sin is when people refuse to believe in Jesus and to follow Him. Justice refers to the fact that Jesus was going to the Father, and His disciples would not see Him anymore. Condemnation, in this context, means that Jesus was going to the cross. Next, Jesus says, "I have yet many things to say to you, but you cannot bear them now. When the Spirit of truth comes, he will guide you into all the truth; for he will not speak on his own authority, but whatever he hears he will speak, and he will declare to you the things that are to come. He will glorify me, for he will take what is mine and declare it to you" (Jn 16:12–14). The Spirit of God, according to Jesus, is going to lead us to truth. Truth is something men must search for. I always challenge men to seek truth more than anything.

I like to challenge people. I ask them, "Why do you believe? Why are you a Christian?" Often I hear, "Because when I was a baby my mom and dad took me to the priest and they had me baptized and told me as I grew up, 'As long as you live in this house, this is what you will believe.'" If that is the only reason you believe, then it is time to grow up. Seek truth. Truth is not always what feels good to you. People often join a certain church because it makes them feel good—but you should never join a church community because it feels good; rather, it should be because they teach the truth!

I received my bachelor of science degree in mental health counseling; my final thesis paper that I had to write was about cults and how people are conned into joining them. Do you know how cults recruit people? They do it by "love bombing" them. They never talk about doctrine. They do not mention doctrine until one is sucked in. They talk and love people into their faith, if you can call it a faith. A cult is formed when enough people say, "Oh, these people make me feel good." Feeling good isn't enough. Feeling good can lead you to hell. We need to seek Truth, and the Holy Spirit will lead us in real truth.

What is truth? Jesus said, "I am the way, and the truth, and the life" (Jn 14:6). If you seek truth, you will come to the feet of the God-Man, Jesus Christ. Jesus goes on to say in John 14:12, "Truly, truly, I say to you, he who believes in me will also do the works that I do; and greater works than these will he do." Jesus Christ told us that if we have faith in Him, you are not only going to be merely a man, but a man who can do what Jesus did and greater things than Him. Can you imagine? Christ will work through us by the power of the Holy Spirit. This God Who lives inside of you made a promise through Jesus Christ, and as far as I know, Jesus Christ is not a liar. He said that we will do what He has done and even far greater than He did!

Acts 1:8 says, "You shall receive power when the Holy Spirit has come upon you; and you shall be my witnesses." We do not receive power so we can be great in the eyes of the world or lord it over others. It is a power to serve. Some Christian men will say, "Okay, I am in charge of my family." Sometimes I just want to whack them over the head and tell them that they are the leader of their family, but not in charge of their family. There is a big difference. To lead your family means you are their servant. Your wife is not there to take care of your every whim. Gentlemen, you are there to take care of every whim of your wife. You are there to die for your wife. You are there to be the servant of your wife. The Spirit of the Living God gives us power to serve, not power for self-promotion. God is in charge of your house.

If God's power makes us witnesses for Him, we must figure out the definition of "witness". In the Greek, the Greek word for "martyr", μάρτυρ, is "witness". Therefore, God gives us the power to lay down our lives. So the power we get from the Spirit of God is to die to ourselves by bearing witness to Christ. Every single apostle, except for John, died witnessing to Christ. The question then is, are you willing to die every day to witness to Christ? Will you lay down your life for your wife and for your children? Sometimes people play games with that. They say, "Yes, I am in charge of the family and they have to do what I tell them. They listen to me." That is not laying down your life; that is being on an ego trip. That is pride. Instead, you must show them Jesus by dying for them. Isn't that great? That is why I say lots of times celibacy can be the most selfish life in the world. I do not have to give up the remote control for my TV. I can watch anything I want anytime I want. Celibacy has its privileges. You have to hand over the remote control, if you are a true servant of your wife. "Here, sweetheart; we will watch anything you want to watch." I am sure you want to be great servants so start tonight and tell your wife, "Sweetheart, let me do the dishes tonight." That might just kill some of you—good.

I want to encourage you to read and reflect on the Book of Romans. It is filled with great insight into God's Spirit, and it will teach you a great deal. In Romans 8:5 St. Paul explains the distinction between the flesh and the spirit; "Those who live according to the flesh set their minds on the things of the flesh." What are the things of the flesh?

They are money, power, and position. These things are all passing. Then Romans says, "To set the mind on the flesh is death, but to set the mind on the Spirit is life and peace. For the mind that is set on the flesh is hostile to God; it does not submit to God's law, indeed it cannot; and those who are in the flesh cannot please God" (Rom 8:6–8). So the question is, do you exist to please God or do you exist to please your boss or anyone else? Do you exist to please the world? It is your decision, God or the world? If you are in the flesh, you cannot please God. However, verse 9 tells us, "But you are not in the flesh, you are in the Spirit, if the Spirit of God really dwells in you." The day you and I got baptized, God gave us His Holy Spirit. God is still faithful. It does not depend on you.

As we have said before, we are saved by grace. Grace is freely given to us whether we were baptized as a baby or as an adult. A baby cannot understand grace, but some adults who have been baptized do not understand it either. They have been given this gift, but they have to open it up. Second Timothy 1:6 says, "For this reason I remind you to rekindle the gift of God that is within you through the laying on of my hands." Now remember, Timothy was baptized. He was a priest. He was a bishop of the early Church. Still, Paul has to remind him that he has been given the Holy Spirit, and every day he has to surrender to the Spirit of the Living God. If you surrender, you will not be bound by living in the flesh.

As I said at the beginning of this chapter, the key to the spiritual life is surrender to the Holy Spirit. Paul knew this, which is why he reminded Timothy of this. So I want to encourage you to decide today to start saying a daily prayer of surrender to the Holy Spirit. Here is a prayer written by Cardinal Mercier, which I have said every day since I was in high school:

O, Holy Spirit, beloved of my soul, I adore You. Enlighten me, guide me, strengthen me, console me. Tell me what I should do. Give me your orders. I promise to submit myself to all that You desire of me and to accept all that you permit to happen to me. Let me only know Your will.

Cardinal Mercier said if you do this, your life will flow along happily—serenely and full of consolation. The submission to the Holy Spirit is the secret of sanctity. It is the Spirit of God that makes us holy.

Pope John Paul II was a great example of what the Holy Spirit can do with a man that daily surrenders himself to the Holy Spirit. I believe he has given us a wonderful example of manhood. He changed the world, and he got his inspiration from his father, whom he called "the Captain". George Weigel writes:

Prayer was something else young Karol learned from the example of his widower-father: "Sometimes I would wake up during the night and find my father on his knees, just as I would always see him kneeling in the parish Church." The Captain (his father) urged his son to pray, daily, the "prayer to the Holy Spirit," through which young Karol came to think of life as vocational.[1]

What would your children find you doing if they woke up in the middle of the night? You need to decide to become a man of prayer, and that prayer needs to begin with surrender to the Holy Spirit!

The Book of Romans states, "Any one who does not have the Spirit of Christ does not belong to him" (8:9). You are not a Christian if you do not have the Holy Spirit.

[1] George Weigel, "Prepared to Lead", http://www.catholiceducation.org/articles/stories_of_faith_and_character/cs0012.html.

"But if Christ is in you, although your bodies are dead because of sin, your spirits are alive because of righteousness. If the Spirit of him who raised Jesus from the dead dwells in you, he who raised Christ Jesus from the dead will give life to your mortal bodies also through his Spirit who dwells in you" (Rom 8:10–11). The Spirit will allow you to live forever. That is a great message of hope. "So then, brethren, we are debtors, not to the flesh, to live according to the flesh—for if you live according to the flesh you will die, but if by the Spirit you put to death the deeds of the body you will live" (Rom 8:12–13). We have to live a disciplined life. The gift that God gave us is His grace, but just like a good athlete, you have to work with those gifts and make them strong. Proverbs 5:23 says, "He dies for lack of discipline."

God also gives us the gifts and the fruits of the Holy Spirit. Isaiah 11:1–3 tells us, "There shall come forth a shoot from the stump of Jesse, and a branch shall grow out of his roots. And the Spirit of the LORD shall rest upon him, the spirit of wisdom and understanding, the spirit of counsel and might, the spirit of knowledge and the fear of the LORD. And his delight shall be in the fear of the LORD." The gifts of the Holy Spirit are wisdom, understanding, knowledge, counsel, fortitude, piety, and fear of the Lord.

In our quest to be true men, let us briefly examine how the gifts of the Holy Spirit animate us and make us instruments of grace. First know that these gifts come from God, not from us.

Let us begin with the gift of wisdom. We will explore this gift in more detail later, but when we talk about wisdom, we are not talking about wisdom that comes from books. We are talking about the wisdom that comes from God. It is a gift of God's Spirit. It is a different wisdom than worldly wisdom.

Do you know people who are so wise in the world, but who are really ignorant in so many commonsense things? Have you ever met people like that? They think they know it all and they have all this knowledge, but they do not have peace in their hearts. Wisdom of the world does not equate to the wisdom of God!

We need to look at examples of some saints, such as St. John Vianney, the patron of parish priests. St. John Vianney was ignorant in the ways of great education. He could not even pass Latin. They were never going to ordain him because they thought he was stupid. But if he was asked anything about God, he could make people cry with his knowledge and wisdom of God. Wisdom of the world can lead to death or it can work into a natural goodness. However, it is the wisdom that comes from the Holy Spirit that helps you to make decisions that are going to lead you to God and to a better understanding of Him.

We need to develop the gift of wisdom to know what God wants. The wisdom of God perfects our speculative reason so that we can know the truth.

If you are a wise person and you are listening to the Spirit of God, you are going to know what is true and what is not true. People may ask you, "Do you think this is of God, or not?" You have to pray about it. There is a Charismatic gift that is similar to the gift of wisdom. The gift of discernment is used to figure out if something is true or not. In every decision we should use the gift of wisdom. How do you fully receive this gift? St. James tells us in first chapter of his letter, "If any of you lacks wisdom, let him ask God, who gives to all men generously and without reproaching, and it will be given him" (Jas 1:5). Just ask!

The second gift is the gift of understanding. This perfects our speculative reason and apprehension of the truth.

Often people will read Scripture then come to me and say, "Father, I don't get it. I am trying, but I just don't understand it." That is why I always tell people never to read the Word of God unless they have first surrendered to the Spirit of God. If you have the Spirit of God inside of you and you surrender to the Spirit of God, then the Scripture that was incomprehensible before becomes self-evident. God in His Word will help you to understand His call for your life.

The next of the seven gifts is the gift of knowledge. This gift helps you to know things that you would not already know. For example, there was a Catholic priest named Padre Pio. When people would come to Padre Pio for confession, he would already know their sins and then he would tell the penitents their sins. Remember, Jesus said, "He who believes in me will also do the works that I do; and greater works than these will he do" (Jn 14:12). Padre Pio would have the knowledge of people because the Spirit of God revealed it to him. Knowledge is but revelation. Peter had the gift of knowledge when the Spirit came upon him. In Scripture, Jesus asked His disciples, "Who do men say that the Son of man is?" (Mt 16:13). The people who did not possess the Spirit of God, if you will, said John the Baptist; some said Elijah (Mt 16:14). Then Jesus looked at His disciples and asked, "Who do you say that I am?" (Mt 16:15). Peter replied, "You are the Christ, the Son of the living God" (Mt 16:16). Peter is right, and Jesus responds, "Blessed are you, Simon Bar-Jona! For flesh and blood has not revealed this to you, but my Father who is in heaven" (Mt 16:17). Peter had this knowledge of God, because God revealed Himself to Peter. That is different than the knowledge of the world. The knowledge of the world will puff you up and give you pride. The knowledge of God will humble you to know the things of God. One way to find out if it is of God or if it is of the Holy Spirit is to know if it builds up your pride or if it humbles you.

The gift of counsel is also called the gift of right judgment. As St. Thomas Aquinas said, the gift of counsel perfects our reason and helps us to move from one reason to another.

The best way to understand the gift of counsel is to determine if it leads people to the truth. Every step we make is a step closer to God or a step closer to hell. There are no neutral steps, gentlemen. Everything we do has a consequence. Everything! Sorry if you do not want to hear this, but it is the truth.

When I need to make a decision for myself or my family I need to ask if what I am about to do is going to lead me toward God or away from God. Then I pray to the Spirit of God. See how practical this is? The Holy Spirit is very practical in our daily lives in showing us how to live. The problem is that most men never ask the Holy Spirit for guidance. Most men just live their lives and make their own decisions. But, a man surrendered to God seeks God's wisdom and takes God's direction. "You lead me, Spirit. Counsel me, Spirit, so I can take the right step." We then need to listen and surrender. This will help us so much with our family and friends. They will come to you when they need help because they will sense that you have a surrendered heart!

The next gift, which we will spend much more time on in the next chapter, is fortitude. Fortitude is courage. It is having the courage to do what is right, to stand up for the truth. Courage is something that men talk about a lot, but not enough men have. Courage means you will stand up for what is right no matter what the consequences, even to the point of death.

In the early Church, many died for the Faith. Nowadays the faithful are targets for gossip and are considered nuts or fanatics. The courage to be a Christian means other people know you are a Christian. People sometimes say to me, "Father, faith is a private thing." No, it is not just a private thing. It's a personal thing, yes, but you are given the power of God to be witnesses. That means at work or in school, you are called to be a witness to Christ. Are you willing to be a witness to Christ even if it kills you? You need the courage of God. Courage is not an absence of fear, is it? Courage is going beyond your fear and taking a stand.

One example is that nowadays when I speak at conferences or do parish missions, I make it very clear that abortion is wrong, and if you don't believe that, then you're wrong. People tell me that I am being awfully judgmental, but I say, "No, I am not; I am speaking the truth." Simple. People write me off or write me nasty letters. However, I will take a stand like that even though it is going to be controversial.

In America, discussing the Church's teaching on homosexuality is considered wrong. The world says we should not go around judging homosexuals, which is true, but we need to lead them to freedom! We need to love them and help them and encourage them, but we can never say that an active homosexual lifestyle is okay.

Years ago when I was a chaplain at Penn State Behrend, there was a large group called Trigon, a gay and lesbian group. Sometimes they would try to debate with my Catholic students, but rarely was it ever productive. One Sunday night as I was hearing confessions, one of my students came in and said, "Father, we are getting killed out there!" because the Trigon group was filming our students and asking them about their views on homosexuality. The students really did not know how to stand up to them without getting mad or in an argument, so I told them to wait till after I was done hearing confessions, and then I would try to assist them.

After I was done hearing confessions, I went outside. They were ready with the cameras and microphones for me. The interviewer asked me, "Father, can we ask you a question?"

"Why, of course", I said.

"Do you believe homosexuals can go to heaven?"

"Well, sure."

"What? Well, do you believe it is a sin?"

"Well, of course. Just like fornication. Sex before marriage is a sin. Sin is sin. I am not here to say one sin is worse than the other, but I will say that sin is sin and God calls us to repentance. I've had three friends who have died of AIDS, all homosexuals. Every one of them was trying to fill up the emptiness inside. The deepest need in our hearts is to be loved, and that is where God wants to meet us. When we go around and try to fill up the emptiness of the flesh, we have to keep doing it because the emptiness grows."

As I was talking to this man in this way, he said, "Turn off the camera." Then he started to cry. He said, "Father, please help me." I then shared with him the freedom found in Christ Jesus.

When you take a stand for truth in love, you can bring life to others. If you and I just go around condemning people, that's not of God. *God wants all men to be saved and come to the knowledge of His truth* (1 Tim 2:4). We are forbidden by God to judge others (Mt 7:1). If we do choose to judge others, all we are going to do is keep them away from God. They will run away from us. If we love them enough and speak the truth in love as Paul says, then we can bring them to salvation. Simply saying, "I'm right, you're wrong", is not using the gift of fortitude.

The gift of piety or reverence means that we come before God with humility. God gives us the gift of piety so we can approach God more purely. What does it mean to live a life of piety? It means that I live a life where God's Spirit lives inside of me and people can see that. I am living God's will in my daily life. You need to ask, "What do You want me to do today, Jesus?" Then you need to say, "I will do it. Give me Your command. Make me obey You." When you can do that, you are no longer living by your power, but by the power of God. That is piety.

The last of the gifts of the Holy Spirit is the gift of fear of the Lord. I love fear of the Lord. However, fear of the Lord is not being petrified of God. St. John says, "Perfect love casts out fear" (1 Jn 4:18). But fear of the Lord is the humble awe before the God of the universe. We read in Hebrews 5:7, "In the days of his flesh, Jesus offered up prayers and supplications, with loud cries and tears, to him who was able to save him from death, and he was heard for his godly fear." When you come to know that you are not God and you come into His presence, there should be awe. Anytime we enter a Catholic church, we have to come to know that we are in the presence of the Almighty God. It is a fearful thing to fall into the hands of God. *He is in control and I am not. I respect Him.*

The best way to look at fear of the Lord is like a child who respects, but fears, his father. The child knows that if he does something wrong, there will be punishment. But, the child also loves his father because he knows his father loves him and would die for him. When we call God Father with the fear of the Lord, we come to know that God is our dad and we have a healthy respect for Him. We will be obedient to Him because we are afraid to hurt our dad. If a person is not deep enough into his spiritual life, he may only be afraid of being punished by Dad.

Let us deal with this for a minute.

Do you think the God of the universe punishes us? Hebrews 12:5–6 (RNAB) says, "You have also forgotten the exhortation addressed to you as sons: 'My son, do not disdain the discipline of the Lord or lose heart when reproved by him; for whom the Lord loves, he disciplines; he scourges every son he acknowledges.'" What does "scourge" mean? To beat! *"He scourges every son He acknowledges."* Aren't you excited? Verses 7 and 8 continue, "Endure your trials as 'discipline'; God treats you as sons. For what 'son' is there whom his father does not discipline? If you are without discipline, in which all have shared, you are not sons but bastards." I love that. What is a bastard? An illegitimate kid. "We have had our earthly fathers to discipline us, and we respected them. Should we not [then] submit all the more to the Father of spirits and live? They disciplined us for a short time as seemed right to them, but he does so for our benefit, in order that we may share his holiness" (Heb 12:9–10 [RNAB]).

There have been many times in my own prayer life when I am in the chapel alone and I am doing my holy hour all by myself, when the God of the universe kicks my butt from one end of the chapel to the other because He loves me and He wants me to be holy. He wants me to be like His Son. It is the same as a parent who has a child and wants his little girl or boy to be good. Parents do not discipline their children out of hate, but out of love. Be humble before God and say, "I will do anything You want. I will trust in You." Every one of us will have suffering in our life. When the suffering comes, can you trust God through the suffering?

Imagine you have a three-year-old son who hates needles. He is petrified of them. Then imagine your son gets pneumonia and needs a shot that will save his life. Your son comes crying to you, "Daddy, Daddy, please don't let that doctor hurt me. Please, Daddy, don't let him give me that shot. Please, Daddy!" What do you do? You hold your little boy while the doctor gives him the shot. Your boy will look at you with eyes that say, "I trusted you and you let that man hurt me." For a moment, he might doubt you, but you knew he had to go through that suffering in order to get cured.

God knows us. He is our Father. He has already seen the end of our lives. When suffering comes to pass, He knows He will be there to hold us as we go through it, but He will not take the suffering from us. Jesus said, "In the world you [will] have tribulation; but be of good cheer, I have overcome the world" (Jn 16:33).

If you and I stand for truth, gentlemen, we are going to suffer. Jesus did. He suffered. That is why we have to come to the Lord submissively, willing to do anything He wants. He is with us and He helps us by giving us His Holy Spirit and His gifts and His fruits.

Galatians 5:22–23 tells us that there are nine fruits of the Holy Spirit: "The fruit of the Spirit is love, joy, peace, patience, kindness, goodness, faithfulness, gentleness, self-control; against such there is no law." The gifts are there as tools to help us to be men, to help us to be children of God. The fruits of the Holy Spirit are the way you can see the gifts of the Holy Spirit operating in your life. They show whether or not you have the Spirit of God living inside of you. Galatians 5 also says, "Walk by the Spirit, and do not gratify the desires of the flesh. For the desires of the flesh are against the Spirit, and the desires of the Spirit are against the flesh; for these are opposed to each other, to prevent you from doing what you would" (Gal 5:16–17).

So if you and I surrender to the Spirit of the Living God, we will cease giving in to the flesh. But we have to make sure we are surrendering every day. The flesh lusts against the Spirit and the Spirit against the flesh. The two are directly opposed to each other. This is why you do what your will does not intend to do sometimes. St. Paul would hold all thoughts captive to the Holy Spirit. For example, if you are having sexual temptation, do not try to run from it. Invite the Spirit of the Living God to capture it. Sin begins in our thoughts, and so does the remedy—the Holy Spirit.

It would be interesting to take a poll of how many people actually surrender their lives to God's Spirit every day. Not surrendering to God's will is like trying to drive a car from Pennsylvania to California with no gas. It's not going to work. St. Paul further tells us in Galatians, "If you are led by the Spirit you are not under the law. Now the works of the flesh are plain: immorality, impurity, licentiousness, idolatry, sorcery, enmity, strife, jealousy, anger, selfishness, dissension, party spirit, envy, drunkenness, carousing, and the like" (Gal 5:18–21). Here, Paul is talking to a bunch of Christians. He continues, "I warned you before, that those who do such things shall not inherit the kingdom of God. But the fruit of the Spirit is love, joy, peace, patience, kindness, goodness, faithfulness, gentleness, self-control; against such there is no law" (Gal 5:21–23). He reminds us, "Those who belong to Christ Jesus have crucified the flesh with its passions and desires. If we live by the Spirit, let us also walk by the Spirit. Let us have no self-conceit, no provoking of one another, no envy of one another" (Gal 5:24–26). Say no to the flesh and yes to the Holy Spirit.

To be a man, we need the Holy Spirit. He shows us what it is to truly be a man like Christ. He gives us power to lay down our lives every day—to be men who come, not to lord over others, but to serve others in love. Do that, gentlemen, and you are going to live forever. Isn't that the goal? So, take courage and be a man who lives in the Holy Spirit.

Three Tasks You Must Accomplish

1. Be a man who daily surrenders to the Holy Spirit. Make a commitment to say a daily prayer of submission to the Holy Spirit!
2. Be a man who uses the gifts of the Holy Spirit. Reflect on the seven gifts of the Holy Spirit and ask God to help you to use them in your life. Take one gift each day for the next seven days and humbly ask God for that gift.
3. Be a man who "fans into a flame" the fire of the Holy Spirit within you. Find a friend, or a priest or a deacon, and ask him to pray over you that you would fully receive and open your heart to the gift of God's Spirit.

Questions and Actions for Reflection and Discussion

1. What has kept you from full surrender to God's Spirit?
2. How can you use each of God's gifts for your friends and family? Be specific.
3. Read Galatians 5:16–26, then reflect about what in you is still in the flesh. What do you have to do to overcome your flesh? Again, be specific.

CHAPTER 5

Be a Man Who Is Strong

The Spirit God has given us is no cowardly spirit, but rather one that makes us strong, loving, and wise.

—2 Timothy 1:7 (NAB)

This Bible quotation is from the old translation of the New American Bible and has since been translated to "For God did not give us a spirit of cowardice but rather of power and love and self-control." The Revised Standard Version, second Catholic edition, translates it, "For God did not give us a spirit of timidity but a spirit of power and love and self-control." I like the original NAB translation's use of the word "strong", because "power" sometimes has negative connotations. But the Greek word translated "strong" in the original NAB—*dynamis*—means "power". It's the word from which we get our word "dynamite". So a strong man is a powerful man, but his power comes from God and not from his physical body or will.

Have you ever seen a big, strong, powerful man with cancer or another disease who slowly started to shrivel up? That man who was so strong became so weak. If the only strength that we have is from the world, we are going to have problems. Our strength must come from God: "The Spirit God has given us is no cowardly spirit, but rather one that makes us strong."

The Preface of Martyrs which the priest prays on the feasts of martyrs, states, "You choose the weak and make them strong." Our strength or power to do what we need to do comes to us from God! He chooses you and He does not want you to be a coward, but wants you to live by the power He has chosen to give you, living your life not in defeat and weakness but in His power and strength!

We have a choice: we can focus on our weaknesses or we can focus on God's strength. We can make excuses every day of our lives or we can say, "Yes, I am weak on my own, but I am strong in the Lord. It is His grace that makes me strong." On a consistent basis we must say, "God, I am weak, but You are strong. Today, Lord, I am not going to focus on my weaknesses; I am going to focus on Your strength inside of me." Every day is a real choice.

To be true men we have to focus on the gifts that God gave us, His strength being one of them. I love what God said to Joshua as he was about to lead the people of Israel:

> Be strong and of good courage; for you shall cause this people to inherit the land which I swore to their fathers to give them. Only be strong and very courageous, being careful to do according to all the law which Moses my servant commanded you; turn not from it to the right hand or to the left, that you may have good success wherever you go. This book of the law shall not depart out of your mouth, but you shall meditate on it day and night, that you may be careful to do according to all that is written in it; for then you shall make your way prosperous, and then you shall have good success. Have I not commanded you? Be strong and of good courage; be not frightened, neither be dismayed; for the LORD your God is with you wherever you go. (Josh 1:6–9)

If you look at every real hero in the Scriptures, you'll find that they all basically were told to take courage and be men, and to be strong because God was with them. So, do not be afraid, because God is with you also. But do not think that you are strong on your own accord. Whenever the pride of strength comes upon you and you think you are strong, remind yourself of your breath of life. It can be taken from you this next second. That thought should give us the proper humility.

Part of being strong is taking responsibility for where you are in your life. Our decisions brought each of us to this moment. Even if you have been dealt a bad hand, and everybody has been dealt one in one way or another, it is what you do with that hand that determines what happens to you. People say, "Father, I am this way because when I was a little kid I was molested. Or I had a bad father. Or I wasn't as smart as the rest of the kids. Or if I only could have been more athletic." Excuses, excuses, excuses!

I always hear excuses about people's pasts. Gentlemen, you will never grow in strength, you will never grow in the Lord, until you take responsibility and start making the decisions necessary for your future. Know that every decision you make is going to affect your future, so take responsibility from this moment on.

A great illustration of this in Scripture is when Peter saw Jesus walking on the water and wanted to go to Him (see Mt 14:22–33). Jesus told Peter to come to Him, so Peter started to walk toward Jesus. As long as he looked at Jesus, the strength and the power that came from Christ allowed him to walk on the water, but as soon as he looked to himself and his weakness, probably thinking, "I am weak, I can't walk on water", or thinking, "Oh my gosh, there is a storm going on", he fell. If we are going to be strong, we can't look at ourselves and we can't look at the situation. We have to look at the Lord and His strength and His power, knowing that we can do anything because it is Christ Who gives us the strength. In Philippians it says, "I can do all things in him [Jesus] who strengthens me" (4:13). Do you believe that? "But, Father, I had a bad past." We can do *all things*. If we believe that, we will always have hope. We can change the world.

My byline for the Reason for Our Hope Foundation is "Your life will be changed forever." Also my radio program is called "Changed Forever". Another host, Dr. Ray Guarendi, once kiddingly asked me, "Don't you think that is a little bit prideful? Couldn't you say 'changed for a week', or 'changed for a day', 'changed for a couple of hours'? You really think people are going to be changed forever?" I responded simply, "Absolutely!"

Now you know, of course, that people don't change because of me; they change because of God. We need to focus on Him, not on His instrument. God can use any jackass, which is why I fit in so well. He wants to use you also, in case you are wondering.

With our strength from God, we are called to have a disciplined life. Another word for discipline is "self-control". In the last chapter, I gave you a verse from Proverbs that said, "He dies for lack of discipline" (5:23). We, as men, need to have a disciplined life. When I prepare couples for marriage, I ask each of them, "Have you been going to church?" Each couple usually comes up with an excuse, the men being the worst. I say to them, "You are not disciplined." It is your choice. If you do not have a disciplined life, you won't grow in strength. A few years ago I was told I was a diabetic and I had to discipline myself. I lost fifty pounds. I worked out. I ate the right foods. I was doing great, and my blood sugar was fine. But eventually I got tired of disciplining myself and dieting. I ate what I wanted and gained thirty pounds. My blood sugar went through the roof. If I die, it isn't going to be God's fault; it's one person's fault—Larry Richards'. Why? I *chose* not to discipline my life. I would have died, if I had continued on that way, so I had to re-choose to live a disciplined life.

It just isn't physical discipline that we need to have; it is more important to have spiritual discipline. Years ago, before I was ordained, I headed a large youth group at Our Lady of Peace Church. One of the kids, who later went on to become a professional football player, called me and asked, "Hey, Larry, do you want to play racquetball?"

"I don't know how to play racquetball", I said.

"That's okay; I will teach you", he said. Wasn't that nice of that kid? He was in college and he was going to teach me to play racquetball.

"Sure, I'll go." I used to work out all the time. So when we got on the court and were just hitting the ball, I thought, "I can handle this. This is pretty good."

The boy said, "Well, Larry, the only way to get good at racquetball is to play a game. So let's play a game."

"Okay, son, let's play a game."

As soon as we started playing, this guy got very competitive. He wasn't going to be easy on the older guy. Bang! He beat me one game. Bang! He beat me two games. I almost won the third game, but I lost. Four games, bang! Five games, this kid beat me. Then he started jumping up and down exclaiming, "You are weak!" I got pretty mad. I shouted back at him, "Oohhh, you beat me. Great. I never played before." It didn't matter to him because he was just happy he could tell everyone, "I beat Larry." So I left to take a shower. It was one of those gyms with group showers. Don't you just love group showers? I was the only one in the group shower and I was almost done, when this college kid, who just beat me five times, comes walking in. As I am leaving, he looks at me and says, "I spend two hours every day working out my body." Whoa! This started to worry me a bit because we were the only two in the shower. He loved to talk about the ripples in his stomach: his six-pack. (He might have had a six-pack but I got a whole case.) He continues, "I've got these ripples."

I stop him there and say, "Can I ask you a question?"

"Certainly", he replies.

"How much time do you spend working out on your soul every day?"

"Honestly?"

"Honestly", I repeat back to him.

He fumbles his words and then says, "Two minutes."

"Two minutes, huh?" Then I ask "Who are you living for?"

He says, "I go to church, Larry—every Sunday."

"Listen, you pagan", I say. "I didn't ask you if you went to church on Sundays. I asked who you are living for."

"I guess myself", he says.

"Yes, I guess so. You work out every day, every day, every day to get those ripples in your stomach, and if you are lucky, darn lucky, you will live to be one hundred, although you might make it as a football player so you will probably die at fifty-five. When you drop dead, they are going to drop you in a hole six feet deep and they are going to throw dirt on top of you, then everyone is going to go home and eat potato salad." I then continue, "I have been around a lot of funerals throughout these years and never once have I heard someone say at the funeral parlor, 'Did you see the ripples on that guy's stomach?' Never once. I'll bet it's because nobody cares. Those ripples will become worm meat very soon. Munch, munch, munch. What about your soul? If you have to work out two hours a day to get ripples on your stomach, how much more do you have to spiritually work out to take the grace that God has given you and become strong in the Lord? How much more?" See, I don't get it. The same men that will spend hours and hours a day working on their bodies, for vanity's sake, will answer my question about how much time they spend praying by saying, "I pray and work out at the same time, Father." Then I have to call them over and whack them with the back of my hand. You have to listen to the Lord. You need to discipline yourself spiritually as much as you discipline yourself physically. You must! The consequence of your failure to be spiritually disciplined is stifling the growth of the grace that has been given to you. Just like you have to discipline your muscles if you want them to grow, if you are going to grow strong in the Lord, you are going to need a disciplined prayer life. Discipline simply means making a decision and sticking to it.

When I started this book I said to all of you that it is time to look at the end of our lives and work back. I hope you took me seriously and wrote down what your goals are. St. Paul wrote to Titus about the qualities that a man should strive for if he wants to be a bishop, but these are qualities that we could all strive for. Compare this list to the list you wrote at the beginning of the book. He should be "hospitable, a lover of goodness, master of himself, upright, holy, and self-controlled" (Tit 1:8). When we look back over our lives from the end, will we too meet those standards as set forth in Titus? St. Paul says we must be "master of ourselves"; then, in case we missed the point, he adds the word, "self-controlled". In controlling ourselves, then, first we are going to need a disciplined prayer time and disciplined time for reading the Scriptures.

One of the things that drives me the most crazy when I deal with many men is that they are too afraid to make a spiritual commitment and to stick to it. Whether it is daily prayer, going to Mass, or helping out at church, they have tons of excuses. Gentlemen, God has given you the power and the strength to follow through and do what He wants you to do, so it is time. The Catholic Church would fall apart if it were not for the woman! Women are the ones who do most of the work in the Church—it is time for you to take your place as a spiritual leader in the Church!

Another thing you will need to do is to be disciplined in what you eat. Right now I kind of hate this, but if I want to be strong physically I have to watch what I eat, too. There is an old adage: "Holiness is wholeness." In Catholic theology, we always talk about how the supernatural builds upon the natural. We need to have a good physical basis, so the supernatural can build upon that.

That doesn't mean that you obsess over eating only good food, but it does mean that you do not become a glutton. Gluttony is when food controls you, instead of you controlling the food. Gluttony is when instead of you eating to live, you live to eat. A disciplined life doesn't live to eat. A disciplined life eats to live. Paul said clearly, "Your body is a temple of the Holy Spirit" (1 Cor 6:19). When we take care of our bodies as a temple, we are doing temple maintenance. We do not do it for our own vanity; we do it for the glory of God. We need to discipline our bodies through exercise. It was not God's will for us to be blobs. Jesus and His friends worked out every day; they walked everywhere. You don't have to go work out every day, but you do have to do something instead of sitting in front of the television set. To be a disciplined person, to show that God lives inside of us, then, we should, as Paul continues in 1 Corinthians, "Glorify God in your body" (1 Cor 6:20). Can we control our appetites? Controlling our appetites primarily means controlling our lusts.

I always lead an examination of conscience for the men who come to my conferences. When I do the examination of conscience, I always spend the most time on lust. I know that this does not surprise you! At a conference recently, the Archbishop of Denver in his homily referred back to my discussion concerning examination of conscience. He said, "You all heard Father Larry. Father Larry did a great job today on preparing all you men for confession. And isn't it amazing; what did he spend more time on than anything else? Lust!" I was standing at the back as he was preaching, but I called up to him, "Bishop, they are all men; what did you expect me to do?" Then the Archbishop replied, "I completely agree. In my experience as a priest over the years, seventy percent of the problems we deal with are rooted in lust. Seventy percent!"

The biggest addiction in America statistically is sexual addiction. Do you know when sexual addiction begins? Statistically in the sixth grade with pornography. Can you imagine? We need to learn to discipline our lusts, and the best way to learn that is as Job says, "I have made a covenant with my eyes; how then could I look upon a virgin?" (Job 31:1). In other words, how could he look lustfully at a woman? In the tradition of the Catholic Church, it is called "custody of the eyes".

We as men, especially, have to discipline what we watch because men are turned on through sight. Women, on the other hand, are turned on through feelings. When women look at pornography, they usually don't get it. Often, when I am counseling couples after a wife finds her husband looking at pornography, she'll tell me, "I think it is disgusting, Father. I want him out!" I then deal with her alone. I say, "This is a very grave problem, and it is a problem that many men struggle with, and we can help." If in the Church it is a big problem, can you imagine how big it is outside of the Church?

To control your body, you must first control your eyes. In order to deal with our own lusts, we have to discipline our eyes not to look at certain things. That may mean that we cannot watch certain commercials on TV. You and I both know that there are certain TV shows that are going to get you excited. Once garbage has entered our consciousness, it stays in. You are what you look at. The more you look at pornography, the more it starts to control you. Then your whole life becomes controlled by that. Jesus said, "I say to you that every one who looks at a woman lustfully has already committed adultery with her in his heart" (Mt 5:28). Every one of us has sexual thoughts and temptations.

One way to deal with our lusts is to praise God when a beautiful woman walks by. When you do this, you are saying, "God, you do great work." But if you look at her with lust and think about having sexual relations with her, that is when you now use her as an object of your lust. In order to keep a pure heart and stave off lust, when I see a beautiful woman I try to picture her as she was as a little child in her absolute purity, and then I ask God to let me see her as He sees her. This helps tremendously!

Today, the computer is the number one source for pornography. You might need to put the computer in a place where your wife or your kids can see you when you are on the Internet. That will help. You have to do those things, because, men, we are all weak. Remember what Jesus said to St. Paul: "My grace is sufficient for you, for my power is made perfect in weakness" (2 Cor 12:8).

If a male dog finds a female dog in heat, the male dog is going to try to mate with that female dog. They are animals. Gentlemen, we are not animals. We were not created like animals. We are created in God's image and likeness!

There are programs that insinuate that man is just another animal. That is a lie. I love my dog, but he is not created in the image and likeness of God—you and I are!

The Church teaches us not to use artificial birth control. Once a guy came to talk to me about wanting to use artificial birth control, using the old argument that God did not want him to have ten kids, did He? I told him, "I don't know how many kids God wants you to have, but have you asked Him? God wants you to cooperate with Him on how many children you are to have, and if the answer is two, then you will need to learn to control yourself more. That might mean that you might have to say no to sex seven days out of a month."

"Well, I don't know if I can do that", he said.

"Well, try staying that way forty-nine years, son, then you can tell me about your seven days a month!"

"Oh, I don't know", he responded. "It is so hard."

See, that is the problem. Most men, especially if they are Catholic, completely disregard the teaching on birth control for one reason: they don't want to say no to themselves. They think, "If I want to have sex, if I have an itch, I should be able to scratch it." They want to have sex when they want to have sex, and they don't want the consequences. That is what artificial birth control does—it stops consequences. It is the most unmanly thing a man can do. He is not standing up for what he is doing; he is trying to stop it.

When I taught high school, kids would come to me and say, "Father, there was a mistake."

"What was the mistake?" I'd ask.

"My girlfriend is pregnant."

"Son," I'd say, "that is not a mistake. That was supposed to happen. When you have sex, babies are the consequence."

Do you know the first command out of God's mouth? Be fruitful and multiply (Gen 1:28). He told us the purpose of sex way in the beginning. Some people say, "Keep God out of my bedroom." Excuse me, but God is the one who gave you the ability to have sex. He is the one who created it; He knows all about how it should be used!

Gentlemen, if Jesus Christ cannot be Lord of your sexual life, He is not Lord of any part of your life. Is Jesus Lord of your sexual life? If not, don't play this game that Jesus is your Savior and Lord. He is not! If He is not Lord of that sexual act between you and your spouse, then how can you say He is Lord of anything else? I hear, "That is between my wife and me." No, Christ wants to be Lord of that too.

Now let us move on to three things you need to help make lust become less of an issue.

First, you need to have a good prayer life. Second, you need to have good friends. And, third, you need to have the heart of a servant. If one of these things starts falling out of whack, then lust is going to become an issue.

We've already explained the necessity of a good prayer life. Lust is trying to fill up any emptiness inside of you. Some people say to me that they are lonely and try to fill their loneliness with fantasy, but the only One who can fill that emptiness is Jesus. If you are only going through the motions in your prayer life, you will stay lonely. However, if you are in a relationship with Jesus Christ and are spending time in His arms every day, then any lustful thought is going to seem like eating garbage in comparison. Once you have tasted real love, everything else is garbage. St. Paul said, "For his [Jesus'] sake I have suffered the loss of all things, and count them as refuse, in order that I may gain Christ" (Phil 3:8).

Do you know Jesus intimately in your prayer life? Do you spend so much time with Him that He is filling up the emptiness? Or are you trying to find fulfillment in other stuff? Lust is momentary happiness that dissipates. St. Augustine, one of the Fathers of the Church, had terrible trouble with lust. He continually asked God, "God, make me pure, but not yet." He loved his lust. In his youth, it was his lust that kept him from being a Christian. He had a child outside of marriage, a son who later became a priest. He struggled, but through God's grace he changed.

Likewise, St. Ignatius of Loyola, the founder of the Jesuits, was a very lustful person. He was a soldier and was shot and wounded. As he was recuperating in a convent, he had nothing to read except *A Life of Christ* and *The Lives of the Saints*—a major change from the tales of chivalry he previously read. After he read these books he thought, "If these saints can be so good, why can't I? If they can discipline themselves, by the grace of God, and become so heroic, what is stopping me?" Then he thought about it some more and said to himself, "Every time I think of lustful things I get intense pleasure, but then it dissipates and I am left empty. But when I think of Jesus I have a peace that never leaves me." Jesus is strong enough to conquer your lusts, gentlemen, but you are going to have to spend time with Him.

The second thing you need in order to conquer your lust is good friends. Men need men. It says in Proverbs 27:17, "Iron sharpens iron, and one man sharpens another." We need each other for mentoring. In our Catholic tradition, we have spiritual directors. But you don't need to have a priest as your spiritual director, only a good spiritual friend. A good friend, gentlemen, is more than just a buddy to have a few beers with. Someone who you sin with is not going to help you grow in the Lord. You need a man who is going to challenge you to be the best that you can be. Ask God for a spiritual friend. You can get involved in a men's group and really commit yourself. When I meet with my spiritual director and he knows I have been struggling with something, the first thing he says to me is, "How are you doing in this?" He forces me to be accountable in my life, especially concerning my sinfulness. Is there anyone in your life who can sharpen you into a great man?

In Luke 22:31–32, Jesus looked at Peter, who would become the first pope, and said, "Simon, Simon, behold, Satan demanded to have you, that he might sift you like wheat, but I have prayed for you that your faith may not fail; and when you have turned again, strengthen your brethren." Jesus said this, knowing that Peter in his weakness would in a few hours betray Him. Do we strengthen our brothers, or do we bring them down and help them to sin? The way we get strength is from other men who are in the Lord. We are called to strengthen our brothers in the same manner as Peter was called. Who in your life are you strengthening? Is there anyone? When you have a strong man in your life—a mentor, a friend—he can help you conquer your lust.

I meet with a group of mentoring friends on a regular basis. I travel a lot, and if I am in a hotel room and temptation comes, I know that I will be held accountable for it. When I return from a trip and meet with my group, they will look at me and say pointedly, "Did you fall to any kind of temptation or look at anything on TV that you should not have looked at?"

"Nope!" I'll say. Why? I might have wanted to, but I knew my brothers were going to ask me if I had given in to temptation. They know me too well. I can't lie to them. I have people, strong men, who hold me accountable in my sexual life. We need men who live in God's Spirit to give us strength so we can face our temptations.

Finally, having a life of service will help us conquer our lust. A life of service means you are not only concerned about yourself, but are concerned about giving your life away for others. Walk to where you have a mirror in your house. Look at your own beautiful face, then take out a sheet of paper and simply write on the paper, "I am third." Then tape that piece of paper onto your mirror. You need a practical reminder of your call to service. Then, before you go to bed each night, ask yourself, "Did I commit one unselfish act today, one act of service?" If the answer is no, you wasted your life in Christ today. You are not a servant. You are more concerned about yourself, and lust is all about you. Lust can't wait to receive. Love cannot wait to give.

What we are really talking about, gentlemen, is we need to use God's power and strength to live a life of self-sacrifice! Let us examine the life of the Father of the Faith, Abraham. The way he became strong was through his willingness to do the will of God, even to the point of sacrificing his son to God. What an act of strength; what an act of faith!

There is a saying, "Sometimes I think I have fully surrendered and then God asks me for something I don't want to give up." To be a man of Christ, to be a true man, you need to live a life of sacrifice!

One of the saints who taught this was St. Thérèse of Lisieux. She died at the age of twenty-four, but she lived her life as a warrior for Christ. Here is a young woman who is calling men to be spiritual warriors! She had what she called "sacrifice beads". Every day she wanted to do at least ten sacrifices for others, so she would use the sacrifice beads to help her keep count. Instead of making a comment or a judgment about a person, she would say something nice about that person then say, "Lord, I make this sacrifice as an act of love for you." Are you a man of sacrifice? Do you take the one life you have and offer it in sacrifice and service? Are you a person who has given everything to God?

Are you willing to sacrifice all things? Is there anything in your life that you would not give up for God? St. Francis gave up his family, every cent he ever made, and even his clothing for God. He walked out naked in front of his father and said, "I no longer call you my father. I call God my Father." Then he left everything to follow God.

Likewise, every single one of the apostles left everything to follow God. St. Matthew was sitting at the tax office when Jesus said to him, "Follow me" (Mt 9:9). He left everything and followed God. James, John, and Peter were fishing when Jesus said, "Follow me, and I will make you fishers of men" (4:19). They left everything and they followed God. To be a man, it is going to cost you greatly.

So often in my own life I think, "Okay, I can play games and think that I sacrificed by not having sex and not having a wife. I sacrificed by not having children too, but would I sacrifice my life for Christ?"

Chapter 21 of the Gospel of John tells us about the three times that Jesus asked Peter if he loved Him; but what the Gospel passage really shows us is what it will cost us to follow Jesus.

> When they had finished breakfast, Jesus said to Simon Peter, "Simon, son of John, do you love me more than these?" He said to him, "Yes, Lord; you know that I love you." He said to him, "Feed my lambs." A second time he said to him, "Simon, son of John, do you love me?" He said to him, "Yes, Lord; you know that I love you." He said to him, "Tend my sheep." He said to him the third time, "Simon, son of John,

do you love me?" Peter was grieved because he said to him the third time, "Do you love me?" And he said to him, "Lord, you know everything; you know that I love you." Jesus said to him, "Feed my sheep. Truly, truly, I say to you, when you were young, you fastened your own belt and walked where you would; but when you are old, you will stretch out your hands, and another will fasten your belt for you and carry you where you do not wish to go." (This he said to show by what death he was to glorify God.) And after this he said to him, "Follow me." (Jn 21:15–19)

If we are going to be men of Christ, then we must follow in the footsteps of Christ. That will always lead us to the cross. It is easy to say, "I'll sacrifice my life for God", but it is so much harder to follow through *every day*. In my own life, I often talk a great game, but I don't live a great game. I need to ask God to change my heart more and more each day, so I can live for Him and not for myself— but this is a process.

Isn't it funny that the things we don't want to do sometimes, like work out every day, eventually make us so much stronger? The same is true in our relationships. When you do something you don't want to do for your wife or kids, it makes you stronger. The sacrifice, though, has to be in concrete ways.

If I were to go to your home and ask your wife, "How does your husband sacrifice for you daily?" could she give me a list? If I were to ask your kids, would your kids say, "I know my dad lives for me. My dad gives me *time* every day. He asks me how I am."

My father would take me out every year for my birthday. It would be just my dad and me. He would buy me a gift, and then we'd have lunch together. My dad wasn't a perfect man, but he was still the best man he could be and I knew that he loved me. He put my needs in front of his own as best as he could. The more you sacrifice, the greater you will be.

Obedience is the next aspect to becoming strong. First Samuel 15:22 says, "To obey is better than sacrifice." If we are going to grow strong, we need to be people who obey the Lord. The best example is Jesus. He struggled to sacrifice Himself. The night he was arrested he said, "My Father, if it be possible, let this chalice pass from me; nevertheless, not as I will, but as thou will" (Mt 26:39). Obedience is better than sacrifice. I used to tell my students all the time, "Gentlemen, the only way you can prove you love God, and know this, gentlemen, is to obey Him. Period!" You can say you love God. You can say Jesus is Lord. But if you don't obey Him, you are a liar. Jesus said, "If you love me, you will keep my commandments" (Jn 14:15). Take His Word and live it.

One of my former students joined the Marines. I recently saw him, but didn't recognize him because I had not seen him in a while. When he was a student, he was this little, skinny youth. Now the kid, with one hand, could throw me against the wall. I said to him, "What the heck happened to you?"

"The Marines, Father", he said. This little, thin teenager became this big Marine. How do Marines turn boys into men? Discipline and obedience. Marines who do not obey can get killed real easily. They become strong in all ways because they learn to obey their superiors. Yet, way too many people refuse to obey Christ. Let this not be said of you.

Finally, as Nehemiah 8:10 says, "The joy of the LORD is your strength." God tells us we can become strong by learning to praise Him. Normally people spend time dwelling on what they don't have. They focus on themselves. They say, "I don't have this or that so I am not strong." Forget about yourself and start focusing on God and His goodness. Praise Him because He deserves it. Start with the little ways God blesses you every day. Everyone has bad days, but try saying, "Thank you, God, that I can talk; thank you, God, that I can walk; thank you, God, that I can eat; thank you, God, that I can see; thank you, God, that I can hear." Rejoice in the Lord and then you will get strong. When we praise God we are lifted up into heaven. Christ's Spirit inside of you will make you strong.

We have been given a gift and it is the gift of the Holy Spirit. The Spirit that God gives us is no cowardly spirit, but one that makes us strong and gives us His power. Now that we have been given this strength, we have to use these tools to grow in strength through Christ.

So take courage and be a man who is strong.

Three Tasks You Must Accomplish

1. Be a man who is strong. Take responsibility for your life and your past. No blaming others. You got where you are because of your actions and decisions and now you can move forward with God's grace by making better decisions.

2. Be a man who is pure of heart. Deal with your lust by inviting Christ into the center of your struggle.

3. Be a man of service. Write out the words: "I am third" on a piece of paper and place it where you will see it every day, and try to live it.

Questions and Actions for Reflection and Discussion

1. Who are some of your heroes who are men? What qualities do they possess that make them strong?
2. Why is lust such a big issue for men in general? Is it an issue for you? How are you going to control it? Be specific.
3. Are you a man of service? How is God calling you to be more unselfish?

CHAPTER 6

Be a Man Who Is Loving

Be watchful, stand firm in your faith, be courageous, be strong. Let all that you do be done in love.

— 1 Corinthians 16:13–14

The Spirit of God makes us loving.

What does it mean for us to be men of love? We love everything, right? We love pizza. We love our families. We love our wives. We love our dogs. We love sports. We have one word that covers all those experiences. But we really need to look deeper into what the word "love" means.

C. S. Lewis explains in his book *The Four Loves* that the Greeks had four words to talk about love: *storge*, *philia*, *eros*, and *agape*.

The first, *storge* (στοργη), means "affection". It is instinctual love. Storge is the love parents have for their children. It is the kind of love that is just built into us. It is who we are. People love their children and have affection toward them naturally.

The next Greek word for love is *philia* (φιλια), which means "friendship". That is where we get the name of Philadelphia, the city of brotherly love. Philia is the type of love that men feel for each other. It is a love born out of a common interest, which is why more men than women love to join groups if there is drinking, card playing, cigar smoking, or a sporting event.

The third Greek word for love is *eros* (ἔρως). It is the natural love of being in love with love, if you will. It leads to God because it came from God. It is the experience of a husband and wife being intimate together, a sexual love. But it is not just sexual love, and it is not a bad love, as it is sometimes portrayed. Even our current Holy Father, Pope Benedict XVI, talked about this in a beautiful way in his encyclical *God Is Love*.

The problem with the first three types of love is that each of them has to do with the self. The person loves someone else, but he is also getting something out of it.

The fourth Greek word for love, *agape* (αγαπη), is what God talks about as charity. Agape is the love of God. Agape is total self-giving, no matter how you respond to it. I love you whether you like it or not, whether you respond to it or not. Agape love, of course, is the love given by God. It begins with God the Father. "For God so loved the world that he gave his only-begotten Son" (Jn 3:16). It continues with Jesus. Jesus loved us so much that He laid down His life for us, His friends, and it is present to us through the Holy Spirit.

We need the Holy Spirit to have true agape love. The Holy Spirit purifies the other three loves so we can live agape love. Now agape love is first directed to God. In Luke, a man asked Jesus, "Teacher, what shall I do to inherit eternal life?" (Lk 10:25). I always love that the man asks Jesus explicitly. Nowadays everyone has his own answer, depending on his particular theology or denomination. I always say, "Let us go to God; let us go to Jesus Christ and see how He answers the man."

> He [Jesus] said to him, "What is written in the law? What do you read there?" And he answered, "You shall love the

Lord your God with all your heart, and with all your
soul, and with all your strength, and with all your mind;
and your neighbor as yourself." And he said to him,
"You have answered right; do this, and you will live."
(Lk 10:26–28)

Salvation, according to Christ, is found in love. There is
a Jewish prayer called the Shema Yisrael, which is said every
day by the Jewish faithful: "Hear, O Israel! The LORD is
our God, the LORD alone!" It is taken from Deuteronomy
6:4–5, "Hear, O Israel: The LORD our God is one LORD;
and you shall love the LORD your God with all your heart,
and with all your soul, and with all your might."

Love needs to begin with God. You can go to church
your whole life and never be in love with God—yes, you
can go to church your whole life and, still, only be in love
with yourself.

Some people have the mind-set that says, "I am going to
see what I can get out of God. God will bless me if I go to
church. God will give me eternal life if I go to church.
God is going to take care of my family and will do these
things for me if I go to church or if I have a relationship
with Him." All those thoughts are focused on the self and
are not true love.

There was a priest friend of mine whose very first confession was that of a nun. When he came out of the confessional box, he knelt down to pray and to give thanks to
God; the nun approached him and knelt next to him and
asked, "Father, do you love Jesus Christ with all your heart,
mind, soul, and strength?"

He was so shocked and said, "I went through the whole
seminary, all my formation, all my years of education, and
nobody ever asked me once if I loved Jesus Christ." Can
you imagine that? The core reality about being a priest should

be that we love Jesus Christ! But I can relate with that priest because I was in the seminary system for over ten years and nobody ever asked me that question either.

How about you? Do you love God? If you do, gentlemen, do you tell Him that? When was the last time instead of just thanking God for what He does for you, did you look at God and say, "I love You"? With all your being, do you desire to show your love for God?

In John 14:31, Jesus says, "But I do as the Father has commanded me, so that the world may know that I love the Father." Gentlemen, the world must know that you love the Father too. People should look at us and know that we are madly in love with Christ! When someone looks at you can they tell?

We prove our love, however, by following God's commandments. Do you try to do everything that the Father has commanded you? That is called being an example, being an example of love to a world that doesn't know love. If you are in love with someone, you will spend time with that person.

On the day we die, I believe that the God of love gives us what we love the most. This is why He gave the commandment to love Him above all else. So let's say you were to drop dead, right now, and God looked at you and said, "I love you so very much and so I will give you what you love the most forever." Would that be Him, and can you prove that by the way you are living your life? If it is not Him, He will give you what you want. If you want anything other than Him, that is what He will give you, which by definition is hell. So every day we need to pray to God and say, "Increase my love for you."

Now loving God is not enough; love for God must prove itself through our love of family, friends, neighbors, the poor, and even our enemies.

Now this love begins with our families, but it does not end there; it must include everyone God brings into our lives. In Matthew 25, Jesus makes it clear that whatever we do or fail to do to others, we do or fail to do to Him (see Mt 25:40). We cannot separate our love of God from love of neighbor.

First John 4:20 says, "If any one says, 'I love God,' and hates his brother, he is a liar." It was Dorothy Day who made this passage come alive for me when she said, "We love God as much as the person we like the least."

Think about the person you like the least. Get a good image of that person. It could be someone that you work with; it could be someone who hurt you, or a person that you cannot even stay in the same room with. As you are thinking of this person, you are probably thinking about how much you can't stand to be around him. Maybe your blood pressure just rose a bit. Well, that is how much you love God!

Jesus even demands that we love our enemies. "But I say to you, Love your enemies and pray for those who persecute you" (Mt 5:44). You see, this commandment to love is not easy; it will cost you your life. That is why we need the Holy Spirit to do it!

How do we live this commandment in our everyday lives? Think of the people who drive you nuts. St. Thérèse of Lisieux would go out of her way to be very nice to the people she didn't like. Now, I'm not good at that at all. Everyone can tell when I am mad. You can read my moods very easily, but that is not the way God wants me to be. He wants me to go deeper and to be more and more forgiving. He wants me to see these people the way He sees them.

I have to make a decision that I am called to love them. It is impossible to love some people in your life, right? Come on, of course it is. That is why we have the Holy Spirit. Get out of the way. Say, "God, it is impossible for me to love that person. But You can. You love that person through me." We have to ask for God's heart. God loves that person we do not like, and He said that person was worth dying for. God created that person; He died for that person; and He loves that person. We are called to have the heart of God and love that person too.

We have to at least allow ourselves to be challenged and say, "I must love my enemies." Not doing so is not an option if we are followers of Jesus Christ. That is agape love.

We sometimes make Christianity very difficult. We come up with all of these other rules. But Jesus, Who is God, gave us only one commandment that we should spend the rest of our lives focusing on. Jesus said, "A new commandment I give to you, that you love one another; even as I have loved you, that you also love one another" (Jn 13:34). And then He makes it explicit, in case we didn't get it: "By this all men will know that you are my disciples, if you have love for one another" (Jn 13:35).

Now let us look at the love Jesus had. Sometimes people make love this "la la" thing. We think of Jesus as tiptoeing through the tulips. We make Jesus this gentle, very peaceful, passive person. Oh yeah, this is the Jesus I want to spend eternity with! Come on, gentlemen; Jesus Christ was a man's man! He gave everything to prove that—just look at a crucifix!

This is one of the reasons I love the Catholic Faith so much. Every Catholic church shows you what love is by having an image of Christ crucified in the sanctuary. St. Paul proclaimed with his whole being: "For I decided to know nothing among you except Jesus Christ and him crucified" (1 Cor 2:2). He said this to remind us what love is.

It will cost you your life. When you say to someone, "I love you", you are really saying, "I will give up my life for you." That is hard. That is the way Jesus loves—total agape.

Some obstacles of love are fear and hurt. "I am afraid that if I let my guard down, I might get hurt." Gentlemen, everybody you ever love will hurt you. Get over it.

Normally your loved ones won't hurt you on purpose, but they aren't going to live up to your expectations all the time. You eventually find out that the person you love and married isn't perfect, which hurts you. "How come you are not perfect? How come you don't want to serve me and cook for me every night and take care of my every need?" You better have a heart filled with forgiveness, because those that you love will hurt you. When you love someone, you are giving them permission to hurt you. When God tried to show us love, what did we do? We killed Him. When we love like Him, others will kill us too.

God wants us to love and, in doing so, give up our lives for the people in our world. First, I want to deal with the poor. We must love the poor. The God of the universe showed us what He wanted of us when He humbled Himself to be born poor. Simple. The Catholic Church has taught us to have a preferential option for the poor. Preferential option means if we see a rich person and a poor person, we should help the poor. So, again, in your life do you explicitly, permanently, consistently take care of the poor?

However, when we are dealing with the poor, we still have to keep our priorities straight. A parish I was once a member of was always concerned about the poor, but they were sometimes not concerned about love of God or devotion to Him. You have to have both. You can't be just a social worker. You have to be a social worker and a lover of

God like Mother Teresa was. Then you can really change the world and help the poor.

How do we lay down our lives for the poor consistently? First of all, that means we tithe. I used to teach my students that if they made a hundred dollars a week, ten dollars goes to the Church or to the poor.

I tell my congregation, "I don't care if you give money to the Church; but you had better make sure you take care of the poor with that money." If asked, I tell people they should give 5 percent of their money to the Church and 5 percent to the poor that God calls them to take care of.

Some people say, "Father, I cannot afford to tithe." I say, "Listen, son; you cannot afford not to tithe!"

What percentage of your money belongs to God? All of it! One hundred percent! God says to you and me, "Listen; let us make a deal. All your money is really Mine. I give you the ability. I give you the thoughts. I give you everything. It is Mine. But, I will let you keep ninety percent. Just give me ten percent off the top." I think that is a great deal!

But most Catholics and other Christians do not think this is a great deal. Even as we tithe, we are only dealing with the Old Testament commands because most Christians cannot deal with the New Testament reality. Read the Acts of the Apostles. What percent of the money belonging to Christ's followers went to the early Church? All of it—100 percent. And then the Church distributed it to the poor. Now, you kind of like the 10 percent concept, don't you?

Financially, do you consistently take care of the poor? And, if possible, with your time? I'm telling you this only because someday you will stand before the God of the universe and He will ask you, "How come twenty-four thousand children of Mine died every day in the world because of starvation while you were alive?" And you might answer, "Well, they weren't my kids." God will say, "Nope, they were Mine. And I gave you an abundance so you could take care of them, but you wasted it all on your wishes, and they died because you were selfish."

We can't say we love God unless we take care of others. James 2:14 tells us, "What does it profit, my brethren, if a man says he has faith but has not works? Can his faith save him? If a brother or sister is poorly clothed and in lack of daily food, and one of you says to them, 'Go in peace, be warmed and filled,' without giving them the things needed for the body, what does it profit? So faith by itself, if it has no works, is dead."

I'm not the one who is going to tell you how to take care of the poor; that is between you and God. I am just telling you that you must.

Men can be selfish, especially in America. We have to remember we are called to live as Jesus lived. Jesus came to serve and to give His life away. It is the same with us. To be a man of love, you must use your talents and resources to build up the Body of Christ, His Church and His world!

In my parish, I have a very strong rule: those who don't work should not eat. This is taken from Paul's Second Letter to the Thessalonians: "For even when we were with you, we gave you this command: If any one will not work, let him not eat" (3:10). I tell my parishioners that there are no takers in this parish, but we all need to do something at least once a year to build up the Body of Christ—everyone does!

Again, we read in 1 Corinthians 12:4–7: "Now there are varieties of gifts, but the same Spirit; and there are varieties of service, but the same Lord; and there are varieties of working, but it is the same God who inspires them all in every one. To each is given the manifestation of the Spirit for the common good." The common good that St. Paul is speaking of is the Church. How do you love your Church, and how do you build it up? There are no lone rangers in Christianity. You cannot follow Jesus alone. He always calls us to a community. To be part of the community means to be a giver, a lover.

After having said all this, we really need to now focus on your family. Blessed Mother Teresa of Calcutta used to tell people to start loving at home first. It does not matter if the world thinks that we are the most loving person there is; the real question is, how do you love your family?

I give retreats for permanent deacons who normally are married. I always tell them, "Gentlemen, your first concern must be to love your family, period. If not, quit the deaconate. Get out." I mean this with all my heart! We need to start at home, or what is the point?

Sometimes people, and not just deacons, serve the Church so they don't have to deal with their families. They think, "I am not appreciated in my family, but I am appreciated in my Church." That kind of thinking can mean that you are not really loving appropriately. You take care of only the people who appreciate you, instead of the people that God has placed in your life.

Husbands are called to love God primarily *through* their wives. Your wife is the sacrament of Christ to you. You are the sacrament of Christ to your wife. When she looks at you, she is supposed to see Jesus Christ. That is why Ephesians 5:22–24 is such a wonderful passage. It says, "Wives, be subject to your husbands, as to the Lord. For the husband is the head of the wife as Christ is the head of the Church, his body, and is himself its Savior. As the Church is subject to Christ, so let wives also be subject in everything to their husbands." Many of us remember the translation that said that wives were to be "submissive to their husbands". The problem is that many men just stop with their wives being "submissive". The men love that part, which is why so many women go crazy.

I make this very explicit when I am preaching at a marriage ceremony. I start with the bride and I say, "Sweetheart, you read the Bible every day, don't you?" At first I usually get a "Yes, Father", and then I say kiddingly, "If you lie to a priest, you know, you go to hell." Then she will usually quickly say, "Okay, no, Father." Then I continue, "Well, there is a verse in Ephesians that says, 'Wives, be submissive to your husbands, as to the Lord.'" And then I ask, "Do you think it means what it says?" And I always get an emphatic "No, Father!" Then I literally jump up and down and scream, "Yes, it means what it says!" When I say this, all the feminists in the crowd become very upset and say things like, "This is another reason I hate the Catholic Church." And the bride thinks, "Why did we ever get this priest to marry us?" I love this!

Then, as anyone who knows me knows, I am an equal opportunity offender, so I turn to the groom, who usually likes all of this. Once I said to a groom, "That will cost you another hundred dollars", and he responded, "That would be the best one hundred dollars I ever spent!" But now it is time for the other shoe to fall. I then ask the groom, "You read the Bible every day, right?" He always responds, "No, Father." Then I ask, "Well, do you know what it says in Ephesians after 'Wives, be submissive to your husbands'?" The groom always shakes his head and says, "No." Then I continue, "It says, 'Husbands, love your wives, as Christ loved the Church and gave himself up for her.'" Then I ask, "Do you know what that means?" I then continue kiddingly, "Your life is over!" Then I tell them that every day they need to be more concerned about each other than they are about themselves! That is what marriage is about!

So you need to start to do at least one unselfish act for your wife every day. Surprise her. When was the last time you treated her the same way you did when you were still trying to get her to marry you?

Next, let us focus on your children, which I think is easier because they are a part of you. Do we allow our children to be themselves? Some people think that the best father you can be is a strong disciplinarian. Absolutely, I agree. But just as much as you discipline your children, you must also build them up.

Sometimes we are just harsh and we think this is what God wants, but that isn't the way God is. God loves us. He gives away His life for us. And then He always tells us He loves us. Correct?

You should underline John 15:12 in your Bible, where Jesus commands us, "Love one another as I have loved you." This is not an option. He also said, "As the Father has loved me, so have I loved you" (Jn 15:9). Jesus told the people He loved that He loved them.

Why is it that men do not do that? Men are embarrassed. They are afraid. It makes them vulnerable. They think to be a man, you don't go around telling the people you love that you love them; but Jesus told twelve men that He loved them. Then He told us to love others in the same way.

Recall the kid who beat me in racquetball. The only thing he ever wanted was for his dad to tell him that he loved him. His father was there for all his games. His father was there for everything. His father was present. He wouldn't miss a game for anything, but he never told his son that he loved him. I can still remember twenty years ago, when I was sitting in my office with this kid getting ready to see a movie, when all of the sudden he got real quiet and started to sob. I turned around and said, "What's the matter?" He looked at me and said, "The only thing I ever wanted was for my dad to tell me that he loved me."

Gentlemen, how short life is. How short. When was the last time that we made sure that our wives and children knew that we loved them? Do we make that our goal in life even when we do not want to be around them sometimes?

Since I came from a family of cops in the blue-collar town of Pittsburgh, Pennsylvania, people often say to me, "Oh, you must come from a holy family, Father." Umm, well, no. Did you ever see the show *Roseanne* on TV? That was my family. Before my father would come home, he would stop at a bar and would get a shot of alcohol and a beer. One of my earliest memories is of my dad and me sitting on a barstool in some Pittsburgh bar and a drunk trying to give me a licorice stick. I remember twirling myself around on the barstool. (I do not think many people in the bar during those nights thought that the kid sitting on the barstool with his dad would grow up to become a priest.)

Anyway, since both my parents were police officers, I got to know many cops. They would come over and spend time with my family. It is a hard life being a police officer— it just is. Every time you get a call, it is something bad. Nobody calls to give you good news.

So growing up with cops, I got to be friends with many of them. As it was, I got to know this one particular police officer very well. This man, though, became a very bad alcoholic. He left his wife and eventually left the Pittsburgh police force and his kids. He moved to Las Vegas because he thought everybody was happy there. He then became head of security at one of the casinos.

He got a new wife, new kids, and a big, blue Cadillac. (Years ago having a Cadillac was where it was at. Nowadays you need a Lexus, a Hummer, or a Denali.) He had everything, but he was still empty. He kept drinking and drinking. After a few years in Las Vegas, he moved to Houston, Texas. He became the head of security of one of the largest hospitals in the nation in a suburb called Katy, but still he kept drinking and drinking and drinking. Just a few days from his forty-sixth birthday, he was dying of cirrhosis of the liver. At the time, I was a senior in college seminary. His wife called me and said, "Larry, he is dying. Can you come out here and be with him?"

"Well, of course", I said. It is a seminarian's duty. We are people of love. Yes, yes. I got on a plane and flew out to Houston. When I entered the room I was not prepared for what I saw. Lying in bed was a forty-five-year-old human skeleton with pure gray hair. He couldn't talk to me because he was on a respirator, but he had a small blackboard to communicate with. I said, "You look like hell." (Ha, ha—I have a negative sense of humor if you have not been able to tell yet!)

He shook his head up and down, but he couldn't say anything to me. I spent a week praying and talking to this man as best I could. He'd respond to me by writing on this blackboard. How depressing ICU rooms can be. At the end of the week, I said, "Hey, listen; I have to go." I had to fly back to Erie because I was a senior in college and it was September. But I said, "You know, I am going to be graduating in May, and it would be great if you could be there with me." The man shook his head up and down, but we both knew this was not going to happen. He was going to die. He knew it. I knew it. So I said, "Okay, I will pray for you." It sounds so holy.

Sometimes we Catholics, we Christians, do holy things, but then neglect the most important things. "I'll pray for you", I said. As I was walking out of the room, I happened to look back because I knew it would be the last time I would see this man. As I looked I saw him desperately calling me back with his hands. I ran around to the other side of the bed thinking that something was terribly wrong. I said, "What is the matter? What can I do for you?" This man took me, grabbed me, and pulled me so close to himself and hugged me so tight that I can still feel it. This was twenty-five years ago, but it feels like two seconds ago. As he held me very close, I said, "Yeah, I love you too, Dad."

The only time I told my dad that I loved him was on his deathbed. Why? Because he wasn't the type of dad that I wanted. Why? Because I spent my whole life judging my father, instead of loving my father.

Jesus Christ, the God of the universe, gave us just one commandment: "Love one another, as I have loved you", and He *forbids* us to judge; but yet we Catholics are sometimes great judgers but not so great lovers! It is time to change!

At some point in our lives, we as men have to get over this. We are sometimes great judgers. We judge everybody: our families; the people we work with; our friends. We hold it up as righteousness. We say, "I am not really judging. I am just saying things as they are." We rationalize it.

My suggestion is when you are done reading this chapter that you go and write your wife a letter and tell her that you love her. Then write to your children and tell them that you love them and why. Don't use this letter in a negative way, by saying things like, "I am disappointed in you, but even though I am disappointed in you, I still love you." STOP THAT! That is a way to control people. Love does not control people. Love, by definition, sets people free.

The way I want you to write these letters is to act as if one of you would be dead by midnight tonight. What would you want them to know?

If you are one of those guys who says, "I don't have to do that, Father, because they already know", let me give you a hint: you will never in your life regret that you told your wife and your kids and the people you love that you love them—never. You won't be lying on your deathbed one day saying, "I can't believe that I daily told my loved ones that I loved them. What is the matter with me?"

I have been to a lot of deathbeds throughout my priesthood, so I know what it is going to be like when you are dying. While you are lying there, the thing that is going to be most important to you is your relationships—the people that you loved and the people that in return loved you. Then why don't we live every day with that in mind?

Some of you ought to write a letter to your parents as well. Don't tell me, "Well, Father, they never told me they loved me." Get over it. You be the first to start it.

Make the decision to never let your wife or your kids go to bed or walk out the door without telling them first that you love them—life is just too short! It will change your family. It will change the world.

As I mentioned, in my adulthood the only time I ever told my father that I loved him was when he was dying. My father, however, did tell me years earlier. In fact, I still have a recording of it. He gave me a cassette tape that recorded a night of one of his drinking binges. I could hear the sounds of the glass and the ice as he was pouring another drink when he said, "Well, Larry, you know, I don't know if I ever said this to you before, but I love you." As soon as I heard this, I had to turn off the tape player, and I have never listened to it again, even though it has been more than thirty years. It is a raw emotion. It really hits the nerve with the essence of who we are.

Every day, I make darn sure that what happened between my father and I won't happen with my mother, who is still alive. You know how sometimes you go to kiss your mother before you leave? My family has never been like that. I let this go on for years, even though I was telling people to tell their loved ones that they love them. One day I said, "Okay, I have to make this real in my family." So one day I said to my mom, "Okay, Mom, I love you. God bless you." Nothing! No return. No "I love you too, son!" Nothing! But I kept persevering for months. At the end of each conversation, I would close with "I love you" to no response.

Finally, a couple of years ago, after doing this for almost a year and a half, I was driving to Peoria and talking to my mother on the phone. Again, before I hung up, I said, "Okay, Mom, I love you. God bless you." And my mom said, "I love you too, Larry." I almost wrecked the car!

We need to persevere with a loving attitude in telling the people that we love that we love them.

It all begins today at this moment. Don't allow your children or your spouses ever to be wounded by you because you were not man enough to love them and to tell them that you loved them.

Make the decision. Don't worry about rejection. It'll only teach you to love like God.

I think the person that learned this most in our lifetime was Mother Teresa. She felt nothing. For many years, she loved the poorest of the poor, and she loved God, though she felt great desolation. When she was younger, she went to God in prayer and said, "God, I want to love like You love." He granted her request. She loved more than anybody we know on this earth. She took care of the poorest of the poor. She washed them; she cleansed them; but she felt nothing so often when she prayed. She would spend at least an hour every day on her knees in prayer before the Blessed Sacrament. She said the Rosary. Even as she was being interviewed, you'll never see her not praying the Rosary constantly, although she felt nothing.

That is agape love. That is a love that gives of itself no matter what. There is no reward required of agape love. You get nothing except to love and to give away your life. When you and I learn to love as God loves, by the grace of God we can start to change the world, beginning with our families.

Take courage and be a man of love!

Three Tasks You Must Accomplish

1. Be a man of generosity. Start tithing and taking care of the poor and your parish.
2. Be a man who tells the people you love that you love them. Write a letter to your family members telling them how much you love them and then commit yourself to tell them that every day for the rest of your life.
3. Be a man who loves your enemies. Start praying for them and asking God to love them through you.

Questions and Actions for Reflection and Discussion

1. People should look at you and know that you are madly in love with Christ! Is this true in your life? Why or why not?

2. Reflect on the saying of Dorothy Day: "We love God as much as the person we like the least." Do you agree or disagree? Explain.

3. Do you tell those you love that you love them? Why or why not?

CHAPTER 7

Be a Man Who Is Wise

Yet among the mature we do impart wisdom, although it is not a wisdom of this age or of the rulers of this age, who are doomed to pass away. But we impart a secret and hidden wisdom of God, which God decreed before the ages for our glorification.

— 1 Corinthians 2:6–7

Charles Dickens once said, "There is a great difference between wisdom of the head and wisdom of the heart."

As we have discussed, 2 Timothy 1:7 tells us, "The Spirit that God has given us is no cowardly spirit, but rather one that makes us strong, loving, and wise." That is from the original New American Bible translation, from 1970. I love that translation; I checked fifteen other translations of the Bible and none of them used the word "wise". According to *Strong's Concordance*, the final word of verse 7 is a noun meaning "discipline" or "self-control". Some modern translations render it as "wise discretion", and "sound judgment" is also used. We, however, will see how wisdom is involved.

As Charlie Dickens told us, there are distinctions between types of wisdom. We are not talking about the wisdom of the world. Wisdom of the world is received through education and book reading. Book knowledge has nothing to do with the kind of wisdom we need. We are talking about wisdom of the heart. We are talking about the wisdom that tells us the way to live. That is why other translations use words like "discipline" and "self-control" instead of "wisdom".

We must first know that wisdom comes from God's Holy Spirit and is a free gift. How do you use your free gift? How do you take this gift of God and make it more alive in your heart? To answer those questions we must go back to where this book started, when I referred to the First Book of Kings. After David told his son Solomon to "take courage and be a man" (1 Kings 2:2 [RNAB]), he died, leaving young Solomon a kingdom to rule. Solomon probably thought, "What am I going to do? How am I going to be a man?" So, "at Gibeon the LORD appeared to Solomon in a dream by night; and God said, 'Ask what I shall give you'" (1 Kings 3:5).

Now think about that, gentlemen. If the God of the universe came to you in your dream and said, "You ask Me for anything you want and I will give it to you", what would you ask for? Solomon, who was told by his father to be a man, replied,

> You have shown great and merciful love to your servant David my father, because he walked before you in faithfulness, in righteousness, and in uprightness of heart toward you; and you have kept for him this great and merciful love, and have given him a son to sit on his throne this day. And now, O LORD my God, you have made your servant king in place of David my father, although I am but a little child; I do not know how to go out or come in. And your servant is in the midst of your people whom you have chosen, a great people, that cannot be numbered or counted for multitude. Give your servant therefore an understanding mind to govern your people, that I may discern between good and evil; for who is able to govern this great people of yours? (1 Kings 3:6–9)

The Lord was pleased when Solomon made this request, so God said to him,

> Because you have asked this, and have not asked for yourself long life or riches or the life of your enemies, but have asked for yourself understanding to discern what is right, behold, I now do according to your word. Behold, I give you a wise and discerning mind, so that none like you has been before you and none like you shall arise after you. I give you also what you have not asked, both riches and honor, so that no other king shall compare with you, all your days. And if you will walk in my ways, keeping my statutes and my commandments, as your father David walked, then I will lengthen your days. (1 Kings 3:11–14)

Solomon didn't ask for any material things for himself; he asked for the spiritual gift of wisdom, so that he could govern God's people. So God gave him not only wisdom, but also riches and a long life too, giving all those things because Solomon was unselfish. The same must be true with us. When we come before the God of the universe and He says, "What do you want?" be unselfish and God will grant your prayer. When we are unselfish, we are showing love and wisdom, which comes from God's Spirit.

We, too, need first to ask for wisdom. God wants to give it to you. He has already given it to you at your baptism and He continues to give it to you in the Spirit. Ask God how to use it. Why? To be a good father; to be a good friend; to be a good business man; to be a good church man; to be a good man of God. Say, "I don't know what to do, but You do, Father. Grant me the gift of the Spirit and fill me with wisdom."

The second thing we have to do is distinguish between the wisdom of the world and wisdom from God. In 1 Corinthians 1:17–23, St. Paul says,

For Christ did not send me to baptize but to preach the gospel, and not with eloquent wisdom, lest the cross of Christ be emptied of its power.

For the word of the cross is folly to those who are perishing, but to us who are being saved it is the power of God. For it is written, "I will destroy the wisdom of the wise, and the cleverness of the clever I will thwart." Where is the wise man? Where is the scribe? Where is the debater of this age? Has not God made foolish the wisdom of the world? For since, in the wisdom of God, the world did not know God through wisdom, it pleased God through the folly of what we preach to save those who believe. For Jews demand signs and Greeks seek wisdom, but we preach Christ crucified, a stumbling block to Jews and folly to Gentiles.

A lot of time on TV we watch people who think they are wise. We have conversations with people with all sorts of degrees and letters after their names. They love to express their wisdom. The more degrees you have the wiser you are, or so goes the thinking in America; but, in my humble opinion, I have found the exact opposite to be true. Sometimes the more degrees that people have, the less wisdom they have. Did you ever notice that? Now, I hope that is not always the case because I'll have my second masters degree soon. We just need to know that the wisdom that we should seek won't come from being scholarly, but from the cross of Jesus.

God chose to reveal Himself through poverty and through the cross. Philippians 2:5 tells us that wisdom is having the mind of God: "Have this mind among yourselves, which was in Christ Jesus." Simple. You will look at things the way God looks at things instead of the way the world looks at things.

Wisdom then has implications with your family, with your money, with politics, with everything—very practical implications. Do you look at your life through the eyes of men, or do you look at your life through the eyes of God? One brings destruction, the other one brings life.

Reflect on Philippians 2:2–3, which says, "Complete my joy by being of the same mind, having the same love, being in full accord and of one mind. Do nothing from selfishness or conceit, but in humility count others better than yourselves." In some translations, it says to let all parties think of themselves "as superior to yourself". Isn't that wisdom? That is the gospel wisdom.

The God of the universe decided to be born in a manger. No one would welcome Him. That is the way that God chose to manifest wisdom. This may be easy to preach, but it isn't always easy to live. Philippians continues, "Let each of you look not only to his own interests, but also to the interests of others. Have this mind among yourselves, which was in Christ Jesus, who, though he was in the form of God, did not count equality with God a thing to be grasped, but emptied himself, taking the form of a servant, being born in the likeness of men" (Phil 2:4–7).

In the Book of Romans, St. Paul refers to himself as "Paul, a slave of Christ Jesus" (1:1 [RNAB]). And in Titus, he introduces himself to everyone as "Paul, a slave of God and apostle of Jesus Christ" (1:1 [RNAB]). Think about that. If you were going to introduce yourself to someone, what would you say? If you heard someone today make a similar introduction, you would think of him as a fanatic. You might say, "That person is really weird." But that is how Paul wanted to be known. He was not living for this world but for the next. He wanted to be known for who he was in Christ, not for what he had done in the world. This is wisdom.

Now to be wise does not mean that you have to say this to everyone you know, but it does mean that if you are going to be a wise man, you are going to have to live it. You are going to have to live as a slave of Jesus Christ!

Often we don't want to even use the word "slave" because it has so many negative connotations and slavery of course is wrong. In St. Paul's time, a slave would always watch the master. If the master went to raise his hand, the slave would be there immediately. To be a wise man means that we are always looking at Jesus to get our orders about what we are going to do next.

For example, when I wake up in the morning, I'm not usually thinking the best thoughts. I have too much to do and it's too early in the morning. Then I do my hour of prayer and refocus myself by saying, "Okay, God, I have a lot of plans today, but they don't matter. What do You want? If You want me to do something different, then tell me."

Years ago, when I was the assistant at St. Luke's Church, I woke up one morning and prayed my holy hour and then had Mass. Throughout the entire Mass, I couldn't stop thinking about how I *needed* to go to St. Joseph's Oratory in Canada. God was telling me, "I want you to leave here today. I want you to go to Canada." I wasn't exactly open to the idea because it was January and it was snowing, and I had a lot of other things to do. I told God, "No, it is snowing. I am not going up to Canada. That's a seven-and-a-half-hour drive. Are you out of your mind? No way!" Finally, after Mass, I could not fight it anymore, so I went to talk to the monsignor.

"Ah, Monsignor?"

"Yes, Larry", he said.

"I had to cancel all my appointments because I have to leave today."

"Where are you going?" he asked.

"Canada", I said.

"It's snowing!"

"I know", I said. "I already told God it is snowing. But He said, 'I want you to go to Canada.' "

So I went to Canada. While I was there, I went to confession. It was one of the most spiritual times of my life because when I woke up that day I had my plans, but God said, "They're nice, but this is My plan for you today. Would you get rid of everything else, please?" And I said, "Ah, okay."

Every day we should start by being practical and having the wisdom of God to say, "These are my plans; what are Your plans? I will do anything You want." That is what it means to be a slave of Christ. It's amazing how many of us say, "Jesus Christ is in charge of my life." I always respond, "Prove it!" Today would you do anything He tells you to do?

First, you have to listen to Him during your prayer time. A wise person is willing to put everything else on the back burner for the will of the Father, for the will of Jesus Christ. Say, "Jesus, I love You; I give You my life." Period. The hardest part of my day is often when Jesus tells me, "Okay, Larry, it is very nice that you have given Me your life. Now prove it. This is what I want you to do today." Two minutes after I've given Jesus my life, I want to take it back.

"Sorry, I am not wanting to do what You want me to do today, God", I say.

"You said you are My slave, Larry", He says.

Yes, we need to be slaves, but we need to be slaves because of love. When you are in love with someone, then you love to meet that person's every need, if it is in your power. So to be a slave to God is to be a servant to Love!

For priests and religious, the hardest vow we take is not celibacy. Celibacy, gentlemen, is an easy vow to take. Trust me on this. Some of you, who are married, already know that. To live a celibate life is to live a free life.

The vow that priests have to take twice, however, is obedience. When I was ordained a deacon I took my vow of obedience, but then when I was ordained a priest, they made me take that vow again. I went to the bishop at the time and asked, "Bishop, how come we have to take obedience twice, but celibacy only once?"

"To make sure it works, Larry", he said.

There is great freedom in obedience. Some people think that the God of the universe just looks at us and says, "I want you to be My slave." That would be a horrible god. Our God says, "Listen, I am going to show you how. I will be a slave to you first to teach you. Now you go and be a slave for others." John 13:1–5 reminds us of how Jesus acted:

Now before the feast of the Passover, when Jesus knew that his hour had come to depart out of this world to the Father, having loved his own who were in the world, he loved them to the end. And during supper, when the devil had already put it into the heart of Judas Iscariot, Simon's son, to betray him, Jesus, knowing that the Father had given all things into his hands, and that he had come from God and was going to God, rose from supper, laid aside his garments, and tied a towel around himself. Then he poured water into a basin, and began to wash the disciples' feet, and to wipe them with the towel that was tied around him.

Verses 12–15 then tell us, "When he had washed their feet, and taken his garments, and resumed his place, he said to them, 'Do you know what I have done to you? You call me Teacher and Lord; and you are right, for so I am. If I then, your Lord and Teacher, have washed your feet, you also ought to wash one another's feet. For I have given you

an example, that you also should do as I have done to you.' "
This is how we live wisdom. We live wisdom by being a
servant to others.

Jesus didn't say, "I want you to be a slave." He said, "You
also should do as I have done." This is the complete opposite of the world. The world has what I call the Burger
King theology. The old Burger King slogan was "Have it
your way." The slogan of a Christian is "Do it God's way!"

Christ never worried about building Himself up. When
He would perform miracles, he would usually tell the
healed person not to tell anyone about what He did for
him. When He did allow the healed person to tell others,
He instructed the person to make it clear what God in His
mercy had done. Jesus Christ didn't want people looking at
Him, even though He was God. We need to follow His
example.

The Jewish people were looking for a messiah to become
king who would set up the kingdom of Jerusalem. They
were looking for, and some still are, a worldly messiah. They
were looking for a messiah who would make the Jewish
nation great. Instead, here comes Jesus, a suffering servant.
That is why many of them could not accept Jesus. He was
the exact opposite of what they wanted and expected, even
though Isaiah had prophesized about the suffering servant
(see Is 52:13—53:12). Some people say Judas betrayed Jesus
because he was trying to force Jesus to be the great messiah
he expected.

The world always wants to know who has the power,
while God wants to know who is the servant.

Let's look at another example—the Roman Empire. Rome
was the greatest nation around. Rome conquered everything. Some of its emperors tried to kill the Christians for
many reasons, but even when they did, ultimately their power

was useless. Many Christians died in Rome, knowing that
this world was not their home.

Rome didn't understand people like St. Ignatius of Anti-
och, who prayed for death: "I want to die. Don't give me
what the world says. Don't try to save me if they try to kill
me. That is of the world. That is not of God. I hear well-
ing up within me the voice of my Father who says, 'Come
to the Father.' " [1] What a way to die!

Is there any better way to die than to die happily? St. Ignatius was praying for martyrdom. "Oh please, God, may
I be worthy of martyrdom." There were the Romans
with their great power, with their great strength, with one
of the greatest armies that ever existed, killing the Christians, but who sits on top of Rome today? The Vatican.
St. Peter's Basilica is right in the same place where they
killed the Christians—on top of the very bones of St. Peter,
whom they killed.

The Romans thought they would rid the world of Christianity. They were fools. God is the wise One. The wisdom of the world may work for a while, but it all passes
very quickly. In the end, God wins.

I like to tell high school students on retreat, "Ladies and
gentlemen, everything you see around you is going to dis-
appear one day. One day all you see is going to be nothing.
All of us are going to be dust." We need to know in the
deepest part of ourselves that this world is not our home;
we are just passing through. Our true home is in heaven,
and we need to do everything in our power to cooperate
with the grace that God bestows on us.

[1] Paraphrased from a letter to the Romans by St. Ignatius as found in the
Office of Readings, *The Liturgy of the Hours* (New York: Catholic Book Pub-
lishing Co., 1975), pp. 1490–92.

That is why a wise person lives for eternity and doesn't live for the world. An unwise person puts all his money in the world. It is a losing bet, gentlemen. Everything you have is going to be gone one day. So what kind of wisdom is that? Are you building treasure in heaven? Jesus says, "Do not lay up for yourselves treasures on earth, where moth and rust consume and where thieves break in and steal, but lay up for yourselves treasures in heaven, where neither moth nor rust consumes and where thieves do not break in and steal. For where your treasure is, there will your heart be also" (Mt 6:19–21).

Money in the bank isn't very useful in the afterlife. Are you giving your life away as a slave? The wisdom of the world says "build, build, build", and "me, me, me". The wisdom of Christ says "you, you, you". Which have you bought into?

Philippians 2:7 reminds us of the nature of Jesus: He "emptied himself, taking the form of a servant, being born in the likeness of men". Did you ever think about that? Do you ever look up into the stars at night and realize that many of those stars in the heavens above are bigger than our sun? The sun just happens to be the closest star to us. There are billions and billions and billions of stars, and the God of the universe is beyond all those things. Yet, this God humbled Himself and became one of us.

Philippians continues to show us God's wisdom. "Being found in human form he humbled himself and became obedient unto death, even death on a cross" (Phil 2:8).

Jesus Christ, the King of Kings, became a slave for you; how could you not want to become a slave for Him?

One of my favorite movies is *City of Joy*. It is based on the book by French author Dominique Lapierre. The book is about a doctor who goes over to the City of Joy in

Calcutta and meets a priest. The priest brings him to conversion of life by inviting him to share the life of the poor. (Of course, in the movie the doctor is played by Patrick Swayze and it is a female nurse who brings him to conversion, but that's Hollywood.)

There is a quote at the end of the movie that is placed on the screen that simply says: "All that is not given is lost." That is wisdom.

Jesus said it Himself, but He said it in another way. He said, "For whoever would save his life will lose it, and whoever loses his life for my sake will find it" (Mt 16:25).

The best way to live a wise life is to live life openhandedly. Let God give what He wants, and let God take what He wants. "God, give me what You want and I will be grateful. Take what You want and I will be grateful."

Job, from the Old Testament, exemplified what it meant to live a wise life. He said, "The LORD gave, and the LORD has taken away; blessed be the name of the LORD" (Job 1:21). Isn't that amazing! Unfortunately, that is a way of life that is foreign to us.

It is foreign to us because we want life to be our way and we want God to make sure that it happens our way. Oftentimes when I am at men's conferences, men will say to me, "Father, I am mad at God."

"Why?" I respond.

"Because He has not given me what I wanted", they tell me.

"Oh. So that is what prayer is, huh?" I ask. Do we think that the God of the universe had better surrender to us and give us what we want? That isn't prayer. That is using God. When we come before God it has to be, "Lord, I am your slave; here are my hands, here is my life, here is my family, it is Yours. Whatever You take, blessed be God. Whatever

You give, blessed be God." It is very difficult to live that life, but that is the best way to have God's mind and to look at everything from the perspective of eternity.

One saint when confronted with the problems in his life would say, "What is this compared to eternity?" This puts everything into perspective.

To make this point more clear, is it better to die at ten or at ninety? Ten, if you believe that heaven is everything that God says it is. If you say ninety, you are looking at the world through the eyes of man. If you are looking through the eyes of God, the ten-year-old is the one more blessed. We must look at life through the perspective of eternity.

I know that you do not remember what it was like when you were in your mother's womb, but I bet that you loved it there! You could feel your mother, and all your life came from her; but you could not see her until you were born. Do any of you want to go back in there?

Well, that is what life is like. We are in the womb of God, if you will. (No, I am not saying God is feminine, but that is another book.) We can feel God; we can experience His love. Everything we have comes from God, but we cannot see Him face-to-face until we are born to eternal life! You got that?

Learning to look at life through the perspective of eternity is not easy. Even St. Peter had difficulties with it. When Jesus talked about having to go off and die, Peter said, "'God forbid, Lord! This shall never happen to you.' But he turned and said to Peter, 'Get behind me, Satan! You are a hindrance to me; for you are not on the side of God, but of men'" (Mt 16:22–23).

When we really take the Gospel and start looking at it from the perspective of what God is saying, we'll notice that He is calling us to an altogether different life than most of us are used to. Jesus clearly states, "If any man would come after me, let him deny himself and take up his cross daily and follow me. For whoever would save his life will lose it; and whoever loses his life for my sake, he will save it" (Lk 9:23–24). This is the wisdom of God.

When we start to stumble off the path of wisdom, we ought to look at Proverbs 9:10, which tells us where wisdom begins. It says, "The fear of the LORD is the beginning of wisdom." Live to please Him. The only thing that should make us afraid is displeasing our Father. If we want to walk in wisdom, we must first ask for the fear of God. Live not for what the world thinks of you, but for what God thinks of you. When we stop looking at the world and start looking at God, then we'll be on the road to wisdom.

Years ago I used to take people to Medjugorje. While there one year, there was a kid from another group who was being interviewed. He was a good-looking and athletic kid. This boy was beginning to live a very holy life, so the interviewer asked him, "What do your friends think about this?" The boy replied, "You know, I was thinking about that and I asked myself, 'Would I rather be embarrassed in front of my friends or before God?' and I concluded that I would rather be embarrassed in front of my friends." What a guy! How about you?

The answer to that question will tell you if you are on the road of wisdom or the road of destruction. I think with all of us it is a struggle; this is why we need to surrender each day to God's Holy Spirit.

Wisdom isn't what you know, it is how you live.

So, take courage and be a man who is wise!

I42 *Be a Man!*

Three Tasks You Must Accomplish

1. Be a man who is wise. Look at life through God's eyes and not the world's eyes. Read Philippians chapter 2. Strive to live your life this way.
2. Be a man of obedience. Start each day asking God what He wants and then obey Him and do it.
3. Be a man who seeks to please God. Too many people are concerned about what others think of them; don't be one of those people.

Questions and Actions for Reflection and Discussion

1. What is wisdom? How do God's wisdom and the world's wisdom differ?
2. How is God calling you to grow in wisdom?
3. Reflect on the saying: "All that is not given is lost." Do you agree or disagree? Why?

CHAPTER 8

Be a Man Who Lives as
He Was Created

*'Let us make man in our image, after our likeness.'. . . So
God created man in his own image, in the image of God he
created him; male and female he created them.*
—Genesis 1:26–27

When discussing what it means to be a man who is created, we must explore our origins. Why were we created? How were we created? In John Paul II's wonderful writing *Theology of the Body* he reminds us that everything is a revelation from God. The naked body, by definition, reveals something about God and something about us. Our bodies were created in the image and likeness of God. To find out a little bit about God, you only need to look at what He has created. The splendor of all creation was man. Before we fell, Genesis 2:25 tells us, "The man and his wife were both naked, and were not ashamed." The way we were created by God is glorious and wonderful. We also read in Genesis: "Then God said, 'Let us make man in our image, after our likeness'"(1:26). Think about that—in the Divine Image you were created.

Jesus, in His Incarnation, takes this one step further. The Incarnation was when God and man became one in the person of Jesus Christ! St. Athanasius of Alexandria wrote, "God became man so that man might become God" (*On*

the Incarnation 54:3, PG 25:192B). It is called the diviniza-
tion of man. This is very ancient in Christian theology.
God reveals Himself through our bodies!

Thus from the beginning God created males and
females—on purpose! One of the biggest problems in society today, in my humble opinion, is when people try to say
there is no difference between males and females! Come
on! There are *great* differences between us—just look—and
this goes way beyond the physical differences. Both males
and females reflect the image of God, but in different ways.
Our physical bodies are very different, but they are com-
plementary, which is a glorious thing. Male bodies and female
bodies fit together; they become a whole person when they
become one. God created us that way on purpose.

Let me pause here for a moment and be very clear—
men are not better than women in any way, shape, or form.
We are merely different. Now that this is out of the way,
let's continue. We have to use the differences in order to
complement the women in our lives. The more we celebrate our differences, the more we will fulfill the women
in our lives. By using our strengths and having the women
in our lives use theirs, we become a whole entity.

Men are not supposed to be like women, and women
are not supposed to be like men—we were created to be
different. As I have been reflecting on masculinity in the
Church, I have found that the problem with the Catholic
Church these last forty years or so is that some new theolo-
gies have arisen that have tried to make men feminine. It is
erroneous to tell men to be overly nice, to be overly gentle, and to speak softly—come on! It hasn't worked. This is
one of the reasons that men don't like to go to church.
Men are not challenged to be better men; they have been
often challenged to be politically correct! I believe that the

Church has been in one of her worst periods since she was founded on the solid Rock of Peter—some people want the Rock to be sand! God forbid!

The problem with too many in the Church these past years is that many of the men have become more feminine and the women have become more masculine! There, I said it; many have thought it, but it needs to be brought out into the open. Men need to be men, and women need to be women, and we cannot be confused! This is the will of God; this is the way He created us! I don't want to be like a woman. I want to be the man God Himself created me to be. Hopefully, you want to be a man that God created you to be also.

Now, as I say this, I must emphatically add that I am not preaching about a man who is some sort of macho man. You don't have to be an athlete to be a man, and you do not have to have big muscles or lift weights or even like sports. You don't need to drink beer or smoke cigars or have a beard, nor do you need to have overly masculine characteristics. What you do need is to be the man God created you to be and want all that entails. This is what we will now explore.

Before the Fall it was the intention of God to make us different. Genesis tells us, "God blessed them, and God said to them, 'Be fruitful and multiply, and fill the earth and subdue it; and have dominion over the fish of the sea and over the birds of the air and over every living thing that moves upon the earth'" (Gen 1:28). Then, "God saw everything that he had made, and behold, it was very good" (Gen 1:31). Notice that only after the creation of man and woman does God say it is "very good". We have to go back to that original innocence in which we were created, because when Christ saved us He transformed us and restored us to the pre-Fall state. As we will see in the next chapter, this makes us holy and this empowers us to be all that God has created us to be.

My license plate on my car reads "UR GOOD". The Catholic Church has always taught that since we were created in the image and likeness of God then we are basically good. We messed up when we sinned, but the blood of Jesus Christ has restored us and calls us to be all that He has transformed us to be. This reality should give you a healthy self-image about being a man. You should not limit yourself to your father, your grandfather, your past, or your lineage. Your history in this world does not define you; your salvation history in Christ, Who created you and lives inside of you, defines who you are.

I speak at many men's conferences with a former NFL great named Danny Abramowicz. He loves to tell the men there present: "Your children will always love their mother, but they also want to be just like their father!" How true this is, but remember who your real dad is—God the Father, so you need to act like God's son!

When you talk to people, you should be giving them an example of the Father of the universe. You are called to give people the image of God because you were created in God's image and likeness. What a responsibility!

This responsibility should bring us to a great humility. St. Augustine was once asked, "What are the three most important virtues?" He responded that the first one is humility; the second one is humility; and the third is humility. Humility means "from the earth". Humility doesn't mean putting ourselves down and saying we are no good. Humility is truly knowing who we are. It doesn't matter if you make a million dollars a year or if everybody thinks you are the most wonderful person; you are still dirt. Remember that and you will be kept humble before your Lord. We are all going to be the same one day—the same! When we realize that we are dirt, we gain freedom.

Genesis, chapter 2, verse 7, tells us, "The Lord God formed man of dust from the ground, and breathed into his nostrils the breath of life; and man became a living soul." We are made from dirt, and sometimes we need to reconnect with that dirt to remind us who we are without God! This is why so many men like to hunt and spend time in the outdoors. It is a way for them to reconnect with something that is at the core of their being, something wild and something untamed. This is part of who we are, but it is not all that we are. We are dust from the ground that has been infused with the breath of God! So there is a part of us that is very earthy, but there is even a deeper part of us that cannot be limited to the earth. Men are always striving for more. We enjoy the quest.

There is something in every man that wants to fight the unbeatable foe, to run where the brave dare not go, to be willing to march into hell like it states in the song "The Impossible Dream"! We were created to be men who go beyond the limits that the world imposes on us. That desire comes from God Himself. He is always calling you to be more, and it is He who gives you the strength for this. We read in Isaiah 40:31: "They who wait for the Lord shall renew their strength, they shall mount up with wings like eagles, they shall run and not be weary, they shall walk and not faint."

One of the roles that men have, given to them by God (see Gen 3:16; 1 Cor 11:3; Eph 5:23), is to be the spiritual leaders of their families. Now this is where I have called men "spiritual wimps" for many years. Many men have let their wives be the spiritual leaders of their families, but this is *not* the way God created it to be. Now this does not mean that you are the master of your wife and family; it means, like Jesus Christ, you are the servant leader of your family. We have touched on this briefly in previous chapters, but we need to take a closer look at what this means.

First off, this means that you lead by example. You must be a man of prayer. For it is only as a son who listens to his heavenly Father that you can bring the will of the Father to your family. You cannot be a good and true leader unless you are a true and good follower. You must daily spend committed time in prayer with God, then lead your family in prayer. Do you have daily committed time with your family in prayer? And no, grace before meals is not enough!

You need to be the spiritual leader by being a man of sacrifice. You exist to give your life away for others, like Jesus did. If you are married that means you give your life for your family first and foremost.

If you are not married then you are called to give your life for those whom you work with and live with and share your day with. You are called to be an example of Christ to the world. When people see you, do they see Jesus Christ?

Some of you are called to be a spiritual leader by being a priest of Jesus Christ! There is nothing better! If you are single, are you man enough to consider if Jesus is calling you to be a priest? We are in such great need of priests. Once I asked a boy if he wanted to be a priest, and he said, "No way, Father; I am going to be a doctor!" I responded, "Why go halfway?" He looked at me and said, "What?" I then responded, "If you become a doctor you can help keep people alive for maybe one hundred years; I as a priest can keep people alive forever!" So please, pray about it—it takes a true man to be a priest—it will not be an easy life, but it will be a life that can change the world for Christ. Just a thought!

If you are married, then another way that you need to be a spiritual leader is in the bedroom. I love to remind men that the very first thing God commands us after He made us is from Genesis 1:28, where He said, "Be fruitful and multiply." God's very first commandment to us was to have sex in order to have children. Isn't that great? So God reveals to us why He created sex. Gentlemen, sex was not created just so you can have pleasure and excitement with your wife.

Sure, pleasure is part of it, but the reason God gave you a body that is capable of sexuality is to increase and multiply. The main purpose of sex is mutual love and procreation. God created sex, and He decides what it is about—not you. You have to be open to life in your love life.

In sexuality, a man is the giver, correct? He is the giver of his sperm. Have you ever reflected on what this means, exactly? No? Well then, let's do that now. When a man gives his wife his sperm, he is saying to her, "I give you my life. Inside of my sperm is all that I am." The woman opens herself up to the man and is surrendering to him. As givers, men are self-sacrificing. We are called to be the instigator, the giver, the one who gives everything in love. This is the beauty of the way God created sex. He made the act of sex an act of self-sacrifice.

This is one reason that artificial birth control is a lie. If you use an artificial means, such as a prophylactic, you are saying, "Here, sweetheart; I am not giving you what I have inside of me. I just want pleasure at this moment, but I don't want to give you all that I am."

The Book of Genesis tells of the sin of onanism. It used to be if a man died without any children, then his brother had to take his wife. One woman got married six or seven times and every one of her husbands died. The last brother, Onan, didn't want to have children with his brother's wife for whatever reason, so when he had intercourse with her, he spilled his seed on the ground. That is called the sin of onanism. God immediately killed him because Onan did not share that which was inside of him. He did not give everything to his wife. Likewise, artificial birth control eliminates total self-sacrificing. Sex according to God's will means saying, "Okay, I am going to give myself to you and then we are going to see where God leads us." This does not mean that you have to have twenty children, but it does mean that you cooperate with God and ask Him how many He wants you to have.

Men are very sexual beings, and because of this, men need to reflect on their sexual lives. "What does it mean to be a sexual person?" "How does God want me to use my sexuality for His glory?" "How am I called to control myself sexually?" "How can I invite the Creator of sex into the very act He created?" "How am I God's instrument when I am having sex with my wife?" All these are questions to explore if you are going to grow in being the man you were created to be.

If you want great sex with your wife, pray with your wife before you have sex with her. I know, you're saying, "Father, don't you think that will kill the moment?" No, it won't. Gentlemen, if you think praying with your wife before sex is going to kill the moment you don't know what prayer or sex is! You are inviting God, Who created sex, to be part of that moment. So I encourage you to pray with your wife before sex. Any dog can have sex, which is no big deal; but only a true man can share his soul with his wife, which always involves participation in the mystery of God. Try it!

Make each sexual act with your wife an act of purity and self-giving. God did not create sex to be lustful. That is why Adam and Eve could be naked without shame with each other. Both of them were more concerned with giving their lives for the good of the other than with taking pleasure for themselves. He created sex to be a gift of self, where one is always more concerned about the other. Like the old adage says, "Love can't wait to give; lust can't wait to get!" Are you in love or in lust with your wife?

Men's responsibilities, however, go beyond the bedroom.

Men today often do not want to take responsibility for their own actions. This is nothing new, of course. Adam did the same thing in Genesis when he blamed the whole Fall on his wife, Eve. In Genesis 3:12 he said, "The woman whom you gave to be with me, she gave me fruit of the tree, and I ate." Notice how Adam even tries to blame God Himself when he says "whom you gave to be with me".

As we said in chapter 5, to be a man of God you need to take responsibility for your actions! That means that you stop placing the blame on society, on your past, on your boss, on your family, or on God and begin to take ownership of the fact that you are where you are today because of the decisions that *you* have made! It is time, gentlemen!

Once you do this it will be good news, because now you can do something with God to create a better future. But start now. Take responsibility for your life and turn it over to Jesus Christ. He will deliver you from yourself and He will help you be the man you are called to be, but only if you suck it up and stop blaming everyone but yourself.

When you turn everything over to Christ and ask Him to make you a true man, then He will begin by turning you toward His Father. This is where He learned to be a man, by loving His Father. Jesus said, "I *do as the Father* has commanded me, so that the world may know that I love the Father" (Jn 14:31; italics mine). When you decide that you are going to look at God, and not the world, and do as He commands, then you begin to live as Jesus lived.

God has chosen each of you to love Him above all things. Why did God love David so much? We read in 1 Samuel 13:14 why King David was chosen. It says, "The LORD has sought out a man after his own heart." To be men is to seek the desires inside of the heart of God. St. Paul repeats this in Acts 13:22: "I have found in David, the son of Jesse, a man after my heart, who will do all my will." Are you a man after God's own heart? Is your primary desire to make God happy?

I once had a very honest man come to me in confession; before we started he said, "Father, I have to confess that I have not been a man. I haven't been a man after God's own heart." What insight!

You have to understand that God used David as His instrument although David was very weak. David wasn't always manly. He fell, like we often fall. What made God choose David was not David's strength, but his desire to fulfill the will of God. How glorious it would be to have God tell us that we are men after His own heart.

As I have said, Jesus was the ultimate man. He, too, wanted the will of God, but He never fell. Jesus loved to challenge His twelve apostles to be better. Men love to be challenged! They will even endure suffering to reach goals. For instance, athletes go through major training to be the best they can be. St. Paul tells us, "Do you not know that in a race all the runners compete, but only one receives the prize? So run that you may obtain it. Every athlete exercises self-control in all things. They do it to receive a perishable wreath, but we an imperishable" (1 Cor 9:24–25).

Jesus Christ is inviting you to run for the imperishable crown of eternal life. By His grace, you will need to work hard for it and be the best man you can be. You will need to mature. One of the big differences between a man and a boy is a man knows that he sometimes has to accept suffering for the greater good. It is a sign of maturity to be able to deny the moment with the knowledge that something good will come out of it. Unfortunately, some men never mature.

St. Paul again calls young Timothy to become a man when he says in 1 Timothy 4:7–8, "Train yourself in godliness; for while bodily training is of some value, godliness is of value in every way, as it holds promise for the present life and also for the life to come." Training in devotion will benefit your life now and eternally. This means that you need to learn to discipline yourself to be a man of prayer and integrity.

Recently I was speaking at a priest conference and I said, "Fathers, God is calling you to be men, and that means that you are going to start giving God an hour a day, every day, by spending time with Jesus in the Blessed Sacrament." Many of them looked at me like I was crazy. I challenged them to an hour; what is God challenging you to do to train you for a life of piety? We need to stop making excuses for our spiritual lives and ask God what He wants of us, and then by His grace, do it.

Shortly after the priest conference, one of my students asked me if we could get lunch. This boy is not Catholic, but has always been like a son to me. When he got in my car, the first thing he said was, "Father, you are going to be mad."

"Son, me mad?" I said then added, "Did you get your girlfriend pregnant?" I always ask first if someone's pregnant, but I never get mad about that because there is a life at stake that needs to be taken care of.

"No, no, no," he said, "but you are still going to be mad."

"Why am I going to be mad, then?"

"My girlfriend moved in with me", he said, then ducked just in case I was going to throw a punch at him.

"I am mad!" I yelled, but showed remarkable constraint in not blackening his eye. Instead, for the next hour and a half, I challenged him to be the man of God that he is called to be. I said, "Son, why would you say that you love her so much, and then you would put her soul in danger of damnation by having sex with her?"

"Oh well, ah . . .", he mumbled.

"The wages of sin is death" (Rom 6:23), I said. "Now listen, you are the man. You are the spiritual leader in your relationship." That is part of the reality. The Word of God says that we are called to be the spiritual leader of our households. Unfortunately, most men hesitate on this point. I continued, "Son, how will you ever be the spiritual head of your household when God blesses you with children, when you have to tell your kids that for three years you lived with their mother and weren't concerned about her soul? You were more concerned about having sexual pleasure. The Bible says, 'No fornicator will inherit the kingdom of God' (1 Cor 6:9). I am not making this stuff up!" Finally, I said, "Son, you have to be a man. Stop making excuses."

After about an hour and fifteen minutes he said, "I guess I have to be a man."

"Yep, you got to be a man!"

Before he left, he said, "Father, please keep challenging me. Please. Keep challenging me to be the man that God calls me to be."

What a great thing that although this kid was a sinful kid and he knew he was risking death by talking to me, he was still man enough because in his heart of hearts he knew what he was doing was wrong. Before he left, out of curiosity, I asked him, "What did your parents say about you moving in with your girlfriend?"

"They are not happy about it, but they don't have any problem with it", he said.

I cried inside. Then I told him why I challenged him. "Son, I love you enough to tell you the truth."

We need to speak the truth in love. Do you love people enough to tell them the truth, even if it is not popular? Challenge the ones you love.

Even as I was challenging and chastising the kid I had lunch with, I never stopped loving him for a second. I never judged him either. I was judging what he did, and I loved him enough to tell him to stop.

Do you live a life of integrity? To be a man of integrity means that you are who you are no matter where you are! This means that you act the same way at church and at work and with your family and when you are alone. The world needs men of integrity! A man of integrity is irreproachable. That is character. True character is who you are when nobody is looking.

Finally, men need men. When I taught at Cathedral Prep High School, I had a weekly prayer group for the boys of the school. Our group was called Fratres Tui ("strengthen your brothers"). It was taken from Luke 22:32 when Jesus looked at St. Peter and said, "But I have prayed for you that your faith may not fail; and when you have turned again, strengthen your brethren." Jesus sent the disciples out two by two on purpose. Men need men to challenge them to be the best that they can be.

Men by nature are very competitive. So when one man can challenge his brother in love to be the man God wants him to be, then he can grow. St. Paul was that type of mentor to young Timothy and Titus. Jesus had His disciples around Him. When He suffered in the Garden of Gethsemane He needed His friends to support Him and be with Him! If Jesus, Who is God, needs men around Him, then who are you to think that you do not? As I said in chapter 5, you need at least one man whom you can talk to, and look straight in the eye and be honest with. You need a friend who will love you as you are, but love you so much that he will never leave you there.

Do you have a friend like this? If not, then ask God for a friend who is a true man of God who will walk with you on your journey to be a man. Find a group of men that you can share with and pray with and will be with you through the tough times. Jesus, in His humanity, needed men in His life, and so do you. It is with them that God will form you and challenge you and love you.

So, take courage and be the man that God created you to be!

Three Tasks You Must Accomplish

1. Be a man who is a spiritual leader. Take spiritual authority in your family and lead by example. Have a daily prayer time with your family.
2. Be a man who needs other men. Find men who will challenge you to grow in the Lord and make you a better man.
3. Be a man who invites God into your sexuality. If you are married, pray with your spouse, especially before sexual intimacy.

Questions and Actions for Reflection and Discussion

1. When people see you, do they see Jesus Christ? Why or why not?
2. Do you have men who are friends in your life who can challenge you spiritually to be a better man? Why or why not?
3. What still keeps you from being the man God created you to be? Explain.

CHAPTER 9

Be a Man Who Is Holy

Strive for peace with all men, and for the holiness without which no one will see the Lord.

—Hebrews 12:14

Of all the chapters I have done, this is my favorite. In some ways it is the most challenging. This chapter isn't just for men, but for everybody. Holiness is not an option!

As we have already stated, St. Paul teaches us that men are called to be the spiritual leaders of their households. This means, more than anything else, that you are called to be holy. You are the pattern of holiness for your wife and children.

As I previously mentioned, my good friend Danny Abramowicz loves to tell men at men's conferences: "Men, your kids will always love their mother, but they want to become just like you!" If we are not holy ourselves, then our families will not be holy. It is that simple. God is going to speak to men, women, and children, but He is speaking especially to men to help us be His very image.

You are the sacrament of Fatherhood to your children just like St. Joseph was the sacrament of Fatherhood to Jesus. Just as God used St. Joseph to form Jesus Christ in His humanity, so too does He want to use you to form your children. And if you are not married, or you have no children, God still wants you to be an example of holiness to all you meet, just as St. Joseph was. So I would encourage you before you read any further to stop and ask St. Joseph for his intercession for you so you can grow in holiness.

Now, if I were to ask you to write down the top ten goals you have in life, I wonder if "to be holy" would be one of those goals. But the reality is, gentlemen, that this should be the number one goal in your life!

Hebrews 12:14 makes this very clear: "Strive for peace with all men, and for the holiness without which no one will see the Lord." The number one goal in your life must be to be holy. Now it can't be a goal in and of itself, right? If we strive for holiness just for holiness' sake, then it can fill us with pride—"Look how holy I am."

True holiness is a by-product of love. When you are madly in love with God and madly in love with His people, then you will be holy. It is only a by-product. It is not an end in itself.

Peter tells us Who God is and what God asks of us: "It is written, 'You shall be holy, for I am holy'" (1 Pet 1:16). God requires you and me to be holy men.

If we look at the definition of holiness from the Word of God we'll learn that the Scriptures say that holiness means to be "set apart". We are created in God's image; we are good.

But being good is not enough. Nowhere in the Word of God does it say "good people" will go to heaven. It says, gentlemen, "holy people" will go to heaven. If I were to ask you if you were good, I am sure that you would say, "Oh yes, Father. I am a good person." Well, I am glad. But the real question has to be: "Are you a holy person?"

If you say, "Oh no, Father, I am not holy", I would have to call you over and hit you. Of course you are holy. Why? Because God has set you apart for Himself. Holiness isn't something we do; it is who we are in God. You got that?

Again, holiness is who we are in God. For instance, who or what makes something holy? God does. Let's look at the example of Moses. One day he was walking through the desert like he always did. "When the LORD saw that he turned aside to see, God called to him out of the bush, 'Moses, Moses!' And he said, 'Here I am.' Then he said, 'Do not come near; put off your shoes from your feet, for the place on which you are standing is holy ground'" (Ex 3:4–5 [RNAB]). Ten minutes before, it was just regular land. It wasn't holy ground. How did it become holy? God was present. God set it apart for Himself. When the land was in the presence of God, God made it holy. The same is true with us, gentlemen.

From all eternity God has chosen us to be holy. Ephesians 1:4–6 says, "He [God] chose us in him before the foundation of the world, that we should be holy and blameless before him. He destined us in love to be his sons through Jesus Christ, according to the purpose of his will, to the praise of his glorious grace which he freely bestowed on us in the Beloved." Before you and I were even created, He chose you to be holy and blameless in His sight.

Who we are in Christ is what we are. If I were to ask you, gentlemen, "Are you holy?" what would you say? The correct answer is, "Yes, I am holy, Father, not because of me, but because of Christ, Who lives inside of me. The day I was chosen and baptized, God set me apart as His own. Now I am holy in God."

We need to grow in holiness by first being born again through baptism. John 3:5 says, "Unless one is born of water and the Spirit, he cannot enter the kingdom of God." To be born again is just like when you came out of your mother. You didn't get up and start walking as soon as you came out of the womb; you grew in the physical reality.

The same is true for holiness; when you come to Christ and are redeemed by Him, you have to grow in holiness. You have to become what God is calling you to be. You are holy, but you need to grow in holiness. Want to know how to grow in holiness? The Catholic Church offers you many helps in this regard.

First off, you have all the angels and saints praying for you. You are not alone! We read in Hebrews 12:1 that we are surrounded by this "cloud of witnesses" that are part of the Church Triumphant that prays for you to join them!

The greatest of these witnesses is our Blessed Mother. There is no holiness without Mary! Some men think that they don't need Mary; they say they go "right to Jesus". In doing so they make themselves greater than Jesus Himself! Jesus, by His own divine will, needed Mary in His humanity. As a young child, He needed Mary to change Him, to feed Him, and to form Him. How can we ever say we don't need her?

Just as Mary taught Jesus while He was in His humanity, so she can teach you. Start saying the Rosary every day! Now when you say the Rosary, don't let it be just another prayer that you pray. Let it be a mystery that you live.

When you say the Rosary it is like Mary taking you by the hand and saying, "Come with me and see all that Jesus did for you." Then you walk with her and she lets you see through her blessed eyes what she saw, and she invites you to experience what she has experienced.

For instance, as you meditate on the third joyful mystery you can actually be spiritually present when Jesus Christ was born. You can watch as Joseph and Mary take turns holding their Divine Son. As you meditate on this great event, Mary looks at you and asks, "Would you like to hold Him?" Then you take Jesus, the God of the universe, in your arms and you hold Him. That is how you pray the Rosary!

Mary will always lead you to Jesus; remember her last words recorded in Scripture were "Do whatever he tells you" (Jn 2:5). Great advice, if you want to grow in holiness!

Another great way to grow into the holy man God has called you to be is daily Mass. Now I know some of you just groaned and said, "Daily!" Yes, daily. The Lord's Prayer says, "Give us this day our daily bread", not our "weekly bread". Now I know for some of you this will be impossible, but for many of you it will just require that you wake up earlier in the morning—come on, be a man!

Now if you cannot go to daily Mass, then decide to stop and pay a visit to Jesus in the Blessed Sacrament every day. Even if it is just on your way to or from work, you can stop by a church on the way; you can quickly go in and fall on your knees and say, "Jesus, I love You; please be with me at work today", or, "Jesus, please come home with me." This could take just two minutes, but it could have eternal consequences. You are showing Jesus that you want to be with Him every day.

My grandmother had a little poem that she kept on her bedroom dresser that said, "Every time I pass a church I stop and make a visit, so when the time comes when I am wheeled in (you know, in a casket) He won't say, 'Who is it?' "

I believe that the greatest way for a man to grow in holiness is time spent before the Blessed Sacrament. When I give retreats for priests, I always challenge them to spend a holy hour every day with Jesus in His Eucharistic Presence. I have spent a holy hour with Jesus almost every single day since I was seventeen years old, and I can proclaim first-hand that you receive great graces by being in His Presence.

It is like lying out in the sun. Just by lying there you get transformed; you might not notice it, but others will. The more naked you are the more of you that gets changed. The same thing happens when you come before the Son of God! Just by being in His Presence you will be transformed, and the more open you are before Him the more you will grow in holiness! You will not notice it but others sure will!

Find an adoration chapel in your city; if there is not one, then get some people together and go to your pastor and humbly ask him to start one. Commit yourself to at least one hour a week in His Presence, and if you can handle it, make that hour in the middle of the night, and watch what God will do!

One last thing to help you to grow in holiness is to make sure you receive the sacrament of penance often; once a month is a good rule of thumb. As we talked about in chapter 3, you will be given grace through this sacrament to leave sin behind, and to forge ahead in holiness!

If you do these things God will make you one of His saints!

As I preach, I often look out and wonder how many people are beginning to listen to what I say. How many people are saying, "Okay, my desire is to become a holy man or a holy woman of God, that I become a saint." As the French novelist Leon Bloy writes in his novel *The Woman Who Was Poor*, "There is only one tragedy, not to be a saint."

When I used to take the boys from prep school every year to the Right to Life March, we would always attend Mass in the Basilica of the Immaculate Conception. As you are walking out of the basilica, on its back wall is a beautiful, large cement mural entitled "The Universal Call to Holiness". As we would look at the mural I would say, "Gentlemen, you see that mural? That is your call. I hope and pray that your desire, your goal in life, is to be a saint! I hope that one day they will have to build another chapel that has a statue of you in it."

This is what I wish also for you. That one day you will have the title "St." before your name. This is what God wants for you; is this what you want? You don't have to be perfect for this, just faithful.

It would be a terrible thing if I were to take a chalice that is consecrated for God to hold the blood of Jesus Christ and fill it up with beer. It would be a desecration. It was set apart for God and I chose it for something else.

Likewise, gentlemen, we can live lives of desecration. God chooses us to be holy, and yet we give our bodies and we give our minds to everything else but God. You and I were created for God!

The Church is, by definition, holy. Again, throughout the centuries, and especially in the last ten or twenty years, there are people who only talk about all the problems the Catholic Church has. Is the Catholic Church a sinful Church? Yes! Her members can be terribly sinful, but it is the same with every other denomination—but that does not take away from her holiness!

On March 13, 2000, Pope John Paul II publicly repented for the sins committed in the history of the Church. The Church admitted that her members had done sinful things— she was sinful, yes, but still holy. This is the same for us! We are sinful, oh yes, but still holy and called to grow in holiness. We are all growing into the maturity of Christ.

What we need to do every day is to get out of the way and let Christ live inside of us more and more. In the Beatitudes, Jesus Christ tells us who is blessed. Matthew

5:6 says, "Blessed are those who hunger and thirst for righteousness, for they shall be satisfied." If you do not have that hunger to be holy, ask Jesus for it.

One of the stories that I love to tell when I do parish missions is about my being thrown out of seminary. The first night in the middle of one of my talks I say, "You know, they threw me out of seminary." All the ears go up and the eyes perk up. If anybody was sleeping for a second he goes "Huh?" Of course everybody thinks it was for some scandalous reason. They wonder what I did and are interested to know why. Then I say, "If you want to know why I was thrown out of seminary, you have to come back the last night of the mission and I will tell you." And they all shout, "Boo!"

Normally, when they come back the last night that is their biggest question. Sometimes I forget to tell them on that night, so after I give the final blessing, they all together yell, "Why were you thrown out of seminary?" People always want gossip!

"Aw, come on", I say. "You have listened to me for four nights, eight hours of your life, and you have no idea why I was thrown out of seminary? I was thrown out of seminary because of my preaching."

My preaching instructor was also my formation director. He was a Franciscan of small stature. The first time you preach can be very intimidating, especially in front of someone who is grading you. This Franciscan was getting redder and redder each time I opened my mouth. (Some say I have that effect on some people.) By the time I was done, he was fuming. "How angry could he be?" I thought. "It was my first time preaching!"

My homily that day was named "We Are All Called to Be Saints". It was the first homily I ever gave. As soon as I was done, he pounded the table and said, "First of all, Larry, I don't want to be a saint. Second of all, who are you to tell people they are called to be saints?"

"Ahhh . . .", I said. I was only a lowly seminarian. "Well, don't you think that it is the job of a priest to call people to holiness in Christ?"

"No, that is not the job of a priest. Your job is to tell people that God loves them and that everything is going to be okay", he said.

Perhaps you can tell that I never fully bought into that theology. I do not believe that this is what God wants, not according to His Word, anyway. As I stated earlier, God says in the Letter to the Hebrews, "Strive for . . . the holiness without which no one will see the Lord" (12:14). Everyone is called to holiness. It is not an option.

Be aware: the chief obstacle to holiness is pride, and that is a very subtle thing. The Pharisees did very holy things, but they were not holy. Why? Because they were not in love. It was all about them. They sought holiness for themselves instead of seeking holiness to be more in love with God.

My definition of holiness is very simple: "When God's will and our will become one." That means I am living God's will fully in my life.

The only way our will and God's will can become one is when we become madly in love with God. I want you to reflect on that yourself. Are you madly in love with God? Can people say that about you? Is that what someone would say more often about you than anything else?

Now, I know that this might not surprise you, but you know there are priests that don't like me! A couple of years ago a parishioner of mine was at a party and met one of my brother priests there. The priest asked him, "Oh, what parish do you belong to?"

"I go to St. Joseph Church/Bread of Life Community."

"Oh, Father Larry", the priest at the party said. Then he continued, "You know, there are priests who don't like Father Larry."

"Yes, we know. There are a lot of people who don't like Father Larry", my parishioner kiddingly said.

The priest continued, "But you know, even the priests who don't like him and everybody who knows him can say one thing about him."

"What's that, Father?"

"Father Larry loves Jesus Christ."

After hearing that story, I thought, "Well, I'm okay if that is what my enemies say about me. That is a good thing." Yes, Father Larry is imperfect. Father Larry has a temper. Father Larry has a big mouth. There are plenty of things wrong with me. My faults would fill a book by themselves. But, Father Larry loves Jesus. I wish it would be true that I loved Christ more than I do. It is easy to preach it, but very hard to live it.

Do you desire to love Jesus more than anything? St. Alphonse of Liguori said that if you embrace all things in life as coming from the hands of God and accept them gladly, you will die a saint. The same is true with us.

You must realize that being holy is sometimes going to hurt you. It is going to take you to the cross. It is going to be painful. The more you let Christ live inside of you, the more you are going to die to yourself. That is why there is no holiness, there is no Christianity, there is no loving Jesus, unless there is the love of the cross in our lives. We have to love the cross. We have to embrace the cross. We have to desire the cross. Jesus said, "If any man would come after me, let him deny himself and take up his cross and follow me" (Mt 16:24).

You and I should gladly say to God each day, "I want Your will done in my life today." Then no matter what happens to us during the day, each night we should say, "Thank you, Father, for allowing Your will to be done today."

If we do that then everything that happens in our lives will be from the hand of God—everything except our sin. Our sin is when we choose to follow our will, instead of His. Once you trust that God loves you, then whatever happens during your day is okay because it comes from the hand of your Father.

There is a great man of God named Chuck Colson, who tells a story about Mother Teresa. Mother not only had her order of nuns, but she also had an order of priests and brothers. One of the brothers came complaining to Mother. He was mad at his superior because the superior asked the brother to do something other than he wanted to do, so he got very frustrated. He went running to Mother and said, "Mother, my vocation is to work with lepers. God created me to work with lepers." Mother said, "Your vocation, Brother, is to belong to Jesus. That is your vocation. That means you will do anything He tells you. If you belong to Jesus, you will be His fool."

I often complain to my spiritual director about how busy I am. He will let me go on and on, and then, while I am catching my breath, he'll say, "Larry, God wants your heart more than what you do. Larry, does God have your heart?" I hate that! But it is so true.

As I have said, we are already holy in Christ; now we need to open ourselves up to this reality. If I were to say to you, "I have all of Lake Erie that I want to give to you, but I can only give you as much as you can open yourself to", and then you come to me with a thimble, then I can only give you a thimbleful. If you come to me with a cup, I can give you a cupful. If you come to me with a bucket, I can give you a bucketful. But, if you come to me with a lake, it is all yours. The same is true with the holiness in our lives. We are holy and set apart for God. Christ lives inside of us. The point of our lives, then, is to grow in that holiness by opening ourselves up more to receive that gift from God. Pray. The more we pray, the more we open ourselves to the glory of God. The less we pray, the less we will grow in holiness.

Holiness comes from Jesus, not from us, right? It is like a man who is bitten by a snake and is going to die. Meanwhile, he sees another man who was bitten by a snake three times before and has enough antibodies in him to live. In order for the first to live too, doctors have to take blood out of the man with antibodies and put it into the man who was just bitten. The blood of one man heals another man.

The same is true for Christ. We were in sin, so Jesus Christ took His blood and He gave us a transfusion. It is His blood that makes us holy. Second Corinthians 5:21 says, "For our sake he made him to be sin who knew no sin, so that in him we might become the righteousness of God." When Jesus became sin on the cross, He was bitten by the snake and He developed the antibody of eternal life. When we come to Christ, He gives us a blood transfusion. It is His blood inside of us that gives us the power. Now, we can confidently approach the Father to be set free of our sin.

If you are going to deal with holiness in your life, you have to first start dealing with your sin—not sin that you are defeated by, but sin that you have power over. In Hebrews it says, "Let us then with confidence draw near to the throne of grace, that we may receive mercy and find grace to help in time of need" (4:16). Instead of looking at your weaknesses, look at the strength that comes from Christ. In 1 Peter 1:15 we read, "As he who called you is holy, be holy yourselves in all your conduct; since it is written, 'You shall be holy, for I am holy.'"

Now, you are going to hate me, but I want you to go to James 3:2 (RNAB), where James is very challenging in his letter. It says: "If anyone does not fall short in speech, he is a perfect man, able to bridle his whole body also." James is telling us how to be a man in the fullest sense by watching our tongues. You can control your entire body with your tongue.

Think about some of the things we say. That is why Jesus said, "I tell you, on the day of judgment men will render account for every careless word they utter" (Mt 12:36). Think about what you say to your wife sometimes when you are mad. Think of what you say to your children when you are angry. Imagine if someone recorded you having a temper tantrum with your spouse and if then that got out to everybody. It drives me crazy when people say, "Do you believe what that person said?" Yeah, I do, because I know what I have said sometimes.

St. Paul tells us what we must not talk about: "As for lewd conduct or promiscuousness or lust of any sort, let them not even be mentioned among you; your holiness forbids this. Nor should there be any obscene, silly, or suggestive talk; all of that is out of place. Instead, give thanks" (Eph 5:3–4 [NAB]).

Yep, your holiness forbids dirty jokes. You have to think about your tongue too. Do you tell dirty jokes? Do you use foul language? Do you make sexual innuendos? Are the words you say words God would be proud of? Do your words reflect your holiness?

We need help to stop sinning. If your sin is with your tongue, lust, anger, or any other sin, Hebrews tells us that we can still confidently approach the throne of God because He has now given us the power in Christ to go beyond these things. The Acts of the Apostles reminds us that it is not *we* who make ourselves holy. Acts describes Peter's reaction to being mobbed after he and John cured a cripple. Peter said, "Men of Israel, why do you wonder at this, or why do you stare at us, as though by our own power or piety we had made him walk? The God of Abraham and of Isaac and of Jacob, the God of our fathers, glorified his servant Jesus, whom you delivered up. . . . And his name, by faith in his name, has made this man strong whom you see and know" (Acts 3:12–13, 16). When we grow in holiness, we realize that none of the power for holiness comes from ourselves. It all comes from God.

St. John Vianney was another man's man and a great holy man. He was just a regular parish priest who had a very small parish in Ars, which was in the middle of nowhere in France. Nobody went there. They put him in Ars because they thought he was not very bright. He graduated bottom of his class in seminary. They never thought he could do anything.

When he got to Ars, he said, "Lord, make my people holy. This is the one thing I ask of you. And if they are not holy, I know it will be my fault. But make them holy." He would spend nights in prayer. This humble man gave the most fiery homilies you would ever want to hear in your life. By God's grace this Curé of Ars would attract kings and queens from France to hear him. His church membership grew so much that he had to spend the whole day hearing confessions.

If you ever want to read a heroic life, read the life of St. John Vianney. The devil would set his bed on fire. Fire would be coming up and the other priests would be running into his room to help him out. It was one of those things you see in a movie. His bed would be jumping up and down. Then

St. John Vianney would get out of bed and look at the other priests, who were scared to death, and say, "Oh, that is just the *Grappin*." That is what he called the devil. It didn't scare him at all. He fought the devil every day.

This great saint has given us the way to holiness. If you forget everything that I have said so far in this book remember these words from St. John Vianney. He said, "This is the glorious duty of man: to pray and to love." To be holy, gentlemen, you have to do these two things: pray and love. Focus on these two things for the rest of your life and you too will be a great saint.

Take courage and be a man who is holy.

Three Tasks You Must Accomplish

1. Be a man who strives to be a saint. Ask God for the grace to grow in your holiness.
2. Be a man of devotion. What religious practices is God calling you to start doing? Be specific and begin doing them.
3. Be a man who prays and loves. The world must know that you love the Father. This is done by praying and loving—live it.

Questions and Actions for Reflection and Discussion

1. Do you want to be a saint? Why or why not?
2. How is God calling you to holiness? What do you have to do to help this to happen?
3. Does the way you talk bring God glory or shame? Why does St. James say: "If a person is without fault in speech he is a man in the fullest sense"? (Jas 3:2 [NAB]). How are you doing with your speech?

CHAPTER 10

Be a Man Who Changes the World

Go therefore and make disciples of all nations, baptizing them in the name of the Father and of the Son and of the Holy Spirit, teaching them to observe all that I have commanded you.

—Matthew 28:19–20

For men to change the world, they must start with Jesus. As I have said through this whole book, Jesus is the example of perfect manhood. This perfect man Jesus formed twelve perfectly imperfect men. He chose His disciples in order to change the world. He wants to do the same with you.

There's a story about the time period after Jesus' Resurrection and His Ascension into heaven. In heaven, all the angels could still see the wound marks on Jesus' hands and feet. They all bowed down before Him. Finally, St. Michael went up to Jesus and said, "Jesus, do they know how much You love them?"

"A group of them know", Jesus said.

"Well," St. Michael replied, "how are you going to tell the rest of the world?"

"I told Peter and I told James and I told John and I told the rest of the Twelve," Jesus said, "and they are going to have to tell others."

"Come on, Jesus", St. Michael said. "How else are you going to do it?"

"That is it", Jesus said. "If they don't tell them, then the world will not know."

St. Michael said, "What is your backup plan?"

"There is no backup plan. If they don't do it the world will never know."

Jesus has no backup plan except for us, gentlemen. It is up to us. Jesus chose those twelve weak, sometimes selfish and arrogant men. Jesus chose men like us. He chose all types of men to represent Him. Sometimes we wish we were like someone else instead of ourselves.

In the past, and still sometimes today, I think that I need to change the world—how proud and arrogant that is. My spiritual director used to tell me all the time, "You know, Larry, you did not do God a favor by becoming a priest!" Ouch! But He was so right!

There is a song out by the Christian group Casting Crowns called "In Me". There is a line in that song that says, "How refreshing to know You don't need me—how amazing to find that you want me." God does not need you or me! We are not doing God a favor by being His disciples. But He wants you to help Him to change the world. Jesus tells us, "You did not choose me, but I chose you" (Jn 15:16). God *chose* you. Are you excited?

When I was in college seminary, I had to go to counseling; everybody had to go to counseling in those days. The doctor said, "So tell me about yourself, Larry."

"I am a Peter who wants to be a John", I said. Peter was loud and often impulsive, but St. John was gentle and loving. I've always loved St. John the Apostle. I love the way John did things and how he always talked about love, love, love. Yet, I am Peter. I have a big mouth, which I often fill with my foot. I do stupid things. Can you relate to any of this? St. Peter was a man with flaws, yet God chose Peter to lead His Church.

Now St. John, of course, wasn't perfect either. Although he was the Apostle of Love and leaned on the breast of Jesus at the Last Supper, he also wanted to call fire down upon the Samaritans because they would not listen to Jesus (see Lk 9:54). He had his own struggle with anger, which I, too, can relate to.

Every one of the apostles was sinful. One of my favorite stories of Peter is when Jesus first meets him and performs the miracle of having Peter catch too many fish to hold in his net. Peter fell down before Jesus and said, "Depart from me, for I am a sinful man, O Lord" (Lk 5:8). Aren't we all? But we are also different and unique. You are not called to be like me (I know you are happy about that), and I am not called to be like you (I know I am happy about that). We are all weak, yet God has chosen us men to change the world in the same manner that He chose the apostles.

Think about the apostles; they consisted of fishermen, tax collectors, those who were not wellborn, those who couldn't speak well, and yet Jesus chose these men as they were. These men were not much by themselves, but through these twelve men the world was changed. Was it not? Short of Christ Himself, has anybody changed the world as much as the apostles?

Even as you write the date—now for instance it is AD 2009. That means 2009 years since the birth of Christ. He changed the world, and the way He changed the world was through these weak men. That same Jesus Christ wants to use you to change the world of today and the future. Part of the problem with a lot of men is that their vision is too limited.

Why are so many people okay with the status quo? Christ was never okay with the status quo!

As I mentioned in chapter 3, one of the first words that Jesus spoke when He began to preach was "Repent!" He told everyone that they had to change. That means that they had to grow and become what God called them to be—His sons and daughters!

If we are going to be disciples of Jesus Christ, we need to have the same passion as Jesus to bring people to the reality of who they are. John the Baptist introduces people to Jesus to give them true life. In John 1:35–37, John invites his friends to be Jesus' friends. He says, "The next day again John was standing with two of his disciples; and he looked at Jesus as he walked, and said, 'Behold, the Lamb of God!' The two disciples heard him say this, and they followed Jesus."

Before we can bring others to Jesus we have to make sure that we are truly His disciples. To be a disciple of Jesus means we learn from Him every day. It won't be our ideas that will change the world. It is Christ's ideas. Our job is to proclaim Christ and learn from Christ and be His disciples.

We read on to verse 38: "Jesus turned, and saw them following, and said to them, 'What do you seek?'" That is the question that Jesus asks you every day. They answered, "'Rabbi' (which means Teacher), 'where are you staying?'" In verse 39, Jesus says, "Come and see." So they went to see where He lived, and they stayed with Him.

We have to see where Jesus is and stay with Him. We must learn from Jesus in order to see what He wants us to do. Then we will capture the vision of God in our lives. Did you get that? We need to find the vision of God in our lives! We don't have the power to change the world ourselves, but by the power of the Holy Spirit through Christ we can.

Do you have God's vision yet? If the answer is no, then what I am going to ask you to do is go and spend time with Him in prayer and ask Him for that vision, then put down in writing what God wants you to do, being practical about it. After reading this book, what are you going to do?

The first thing He says is, "Come and see." Practically speaking, how are you going to do that? Throughout this book, I told you to pray every day. "Okay, Father, I have it. I'll pray every day. Read the Bible." Okay, yeah, yeah. Have you started? What are some of the things that you are going to do for the rest of your life? Write them down and make a list of the things that you are going to do now for the rest of your life! That's the point. It has to be for the rest of your life!

The habits you create now have to be lasting. Jesus' apostles stayed with Him for three years, watching what He did and listening to His words. As a result, they were transformed permanently. When you write your list, be specific.

I have written my list for Jesus throughout my life. Some things have been everyday things that He asked me to promise Him that I would do every day for the rest of my life. One of those things happened as I knelt before Him in the Blessed Sacrament at Franciscan University in Steubenville. As I looked at Him in the monstrance, I knew that He wanted me to promise to be with Him every day. So as I knelt before Him I said, "Jesus Christ, I promise You for the rest of my life I will give You one hour a day in prayer. I promise You, for the rest of my life." I have been faithful to that promise because it was a practical promise to God.

Now don't say, "I have done this before and it never worked." Get over yourself and what you did before. Now is your time to be a man and commit to how you will spend time with God for the rest of your life. I recently finished a mission where I really let the men have it.

Afterward, one guy came up to me and said, "Father, you just beat us up. You never let us go this week." I said, "Good! You should be with me when I am dealing with men all the time. This is the reality." Be tough and be accountable in order to better know God. I can't tell you what to write on your list; I only suggest that you start with how you spend your time. If you merely say, "I'll say the Rosary or I will read the Bible", you aren't staying with Jesus. The apostles had to spend time with Jesus to come and see what He wanted. Also, don't say, "From this day on I will *try*." There is no "*try*", gentlemen. You do it or you don't.

The apostles observed Jesus. Isn't that something? They observed what Jesus did and they learned to do the same. For us to be men who will change the world we will have to observe what Jesus did. The best way to do that is by reading the Scriptures. Look at Jesus and say, "Okay, how then must I live, Jesus?" Watch how Jesus deals with people in the Gospels.

You do realize that Jesus Christ would not be accepted in most churches today. They would throw Him out because at times He is harsh—not sometimes, a lot of times! He would go in and take a whip out and go through the Temple area and turn everything over. The apostles were watching Him. They learned that to be men, they had to stand up. Jesus had zeal for the House of God. The apostles must have thought to themselves, "Oh, I must have zeal for the House of God also."

They watched Jesus perform miracles, then they probably thought, "Oh, then I must be a miracle worker too, because Christ Who lives in me performs miracles." He promises, "I say to you, he who believes in me will also do the works that I do; and greater works than these" (Jn 14:12). I don't agree with a world that says miracles don't happen.

I look at Jesus and say miracles are a daily occurrence. Do you believe Him or is He a liar?

You will need to stand up for the truth whether you feel like it or not because He stood up for the truth. You will reach out to the sinners, whom others reject, and will spend time with them because Jesus did. You will be a man of compassion. Why? Because Jesus was a man of compassion.

In order to follow His command to "come and see", you are really going to have to become a man who comes to know the Word of God explicitly and fully. Don't just spend time reading the Bible; come to know Jesus in His Word. Spend time reading the Gospels and learn to act the way Jesus acted. That must be your goal.

As you look at the Gospels and start watching Jesus, try to replicate His actions. Ask yourself, "Do I do what Jesus did in this situation?" Simple. First, however, you must know how Jesus acted.

So, for the next six months, spend time with the Gospels. Start with Matthew, then Mark, Luke, and John. Don't just read, but observe Jesus like the apostles did. Make your goal to mimic the way Jesus lived. I think doing that will be very profound in your life. You will see Jesus in an altogether different light. You will see Him as the example of manhood. As you are observing Jesus, start writing those qualities down that He is calling you to have.

Years ago, when I was in the seminary, I went and had dinner with some nuns, and they said to me, "Larry, you know one of the gifts God's given you, don't you?"

"No, Sisters", I said.

"It is a holy boldness", they told me.

Can you imagine? It is one of the gifts I have. I am a bold person. Not all of us are going to exemplify all the qualities of Jesus, but since we are members of the Body of

Christ and each of us is a different part, each of us will take certain qualities of Jesus and exemplify them.

Over the next six months, as you are going through the Gospels, try to see what qualities Christ is calling you to acquire. Write the characteristics and qualities of Jesus in a notebook. Then ask Him which of those qualities He is calling you to live.

For each of us, it is going to be a different list of qualities. There are certain ones we will all get. For example, we are all called to be men of love, correct? But each of us will be men of love in a different way. Some of you are much more gentle than others when it comes to loving.

To me gentleness is a great gift, but I only have that one in the confessional. It kills me to be gentle. It goes against everything inside of me. It is not part of my style. But often He calls me to let go of my style and at other times He tells me to get out of the way and let Him be gentle through me.

From Jesus the apostles learned how to pray. They asked Him specifically, "Lord, teach us to pray" (Lk 11:1). They were people open to learning. The more you grow in wisdom, the more you know what you don't know. There is always more growing to be done. If St. John and St. Peter could ask Jesus how to pray, why can't you say, "Okay, Lord, You teach me how to pray. You teach me how to be a man"?

Amongst the apostles, Peter was the man. He was the gruff one. He was also sinful. He betrayed Jesus, yet God still chose him to lead His Church. There is very little difference between Peter and Judas except for one reality: repentance. Both betrayed Christ, but the difference was that this one sinful man, Peter, repented. Judas despaired. Some people despair in their following of Christ instead of having a life of repentance. Judas and Peter both sat at the feet of Jesus for years. Even sitting at the feet of Jesus, they still fell. Just because you spend time with Jesus doesn't mean you are going to become perfect. When you and I follow Christ, we are always going to have a life of repentance.

For my first Mass after I was ordained I chose John 21:15–19, which takes place after the Resurrection. Jesus had already revealed Himself, and in this verse He takes Peter aside because Peter had denied Him three times. Jesus wants Peter to feel repentance, but also to feel redeemed. Jesus doesn't just forgive Peter; He restores Peter. Jesus could have said, "Okay, Peter, you can still be one of My followers, but you really screwed up, so you will go to the bottom of the barrel and sit there forever. You can just keep eating dirt for the rest of your life." That isn't what Jesus does. He restores Peter to leadership because Peter had a heart of repentance.

Sometimes when I am out on missions, people think that I have it all together. I tell them to just ask my parishioners. They will tell you that Father Larry can be the biggest jerk ever. They will tell you that I am constantly needing repentance and am constantly needing to be restored by the grace of God.

When we fall, we need to get back up again by the grace of God. The same was true for Peter as we read in John 21:15, "When they had finished breakfast, Jesus said to Simon Peter, 'Simon, son of John, do you love me more than these?'" He asks him the same question three times; just as Peter denied Christ three times, now he is given the chance to reaffirm his love for Jesus three times: "Yes, Lord; you know that I love you" (see Jn 21:15–17).

What do you do when Jesus asks you that same question after you have fallen? Too often when people fall, they say that they are no good and focus only on themselves and their weaknesses. Jesus doesn't do that. He just asks Peter the question: "Do you love me more than these?" (Jn 21:15).

When you go to confession, Jesus asks you the very same question. Peter responded, "Yes, Lord; you know that I love you." To which Jesus said, "Feed my lambs" (Jn 21:15).

It is one thing to say you love God, but God wants you to prove it by ministering to His people. You have to serve. By being a witness and teaching others the truth, you are giving them eternal life.

Part of our job as witnesses is feeding others the truth about Jesus Christ. Are you ashamed of Jesus Christ or is your goal to evangelize and change the world? If Jesus were to say to you, "If you love Me, then I want you to feed My sheep", don't say, "Let me love You the way I want to."

Feeding God's sheep begins with your family, then with your friends and co-workers. Then it goes out to the world. Jesus continues in John 21:18 by saying, "I say to you, when you were young, you fastened your own belt and walked where you would; but when you are old, you will stretch out your hands, and another will fasten your belt for you and carry you where you do not wish to go." John tells us that Jesus was indicating what sort of death Peter would have in order to glorify God. When Jesus had finished speaking to him, He said, "Follow me" (Jn 21:19).

We must go back to the opening line of this book: You are going to die. Now ask yourself, "Will my death glorify God?" Or will it glorify you or glorify what you worked for, or glorify your company? Whom will your death glorify? Jesus told Peter that in order for him to be a man, he would have to serve Christ his whole life. Jesus said, "Follow me." Follow Jesus to the cross.

Gentlemen, the way we change the world is by following Jesus Christ every day, by glorifying God and living practically.

Catholics tend to be very good at being present, but that is only following half of what Jesus commanded when he said, "Come and see" (Jn 1:39). "Okay, Jesus, I'll come and I will be there." Great, gentlemen! But, we have to keep going.

The last words that Jesus gives at the end of Matthew's Gospel concern encouragement. Jesus had been resurrected into His glory and summons His apostles. Matthew 28:18–20 says, "All authority in heaven and on earth has been given to me. Go therefore and make disciples of all nations, baptizing them in the name of the Father and of the Son and of the Holy Spirit, teaching them to observe all that I have commanded you; and behold, I am with you always, to the close of the age." Jesus was going back to heaven and these are His final marching orders. He says, "Go therefore and make disciples." You understand, His apostles already accepted His invitation to "come", now they must "go and make disciples".

As I mentioned in a previous chapter, I came to know Jesus Christ when I was seventeen years old, and it was through a Baptist preacher: Billy Graham. I would love to tell him one day that he was one of the instruments that God used to bring me to Him. I have always had such respect for Billy because the whole purpose of Billy's life was to bring everybody to Christ. He is a man who, by God's grace, has been living with integrity his whole life. He hasn't gotten involved in any scandals. He has made sure that all the money for his ministry was taken care of by somebody else. He was never alone in a car with a woman. He also made sure he had enough people around him, which is always the key, to protect him so he could remain a man of integrity.

I knew that Christ had called me also to be like Billy Graham in the Catholic Church, to bring people to the fullness of the truth, and this is what I live for.

When I wrote my letter to go to seminary as a seventeen-year-old, I said in the letter that I wanted to bring the whole world to Jesus Christ. That is my goal. That is the goal of the Reason for Our Hope Foundation, which I founded. I want to bring the world to a living, loving relationship with Jesus Christ! Everybody!

I am not trying to get people to believe a certain way. I am not here to argue. I want to bring people into a relationship with Jesus Christ. If you haven't figured it out yet, gentlemen, we are salesmen. I am a salesman. I sell eternal life. If you love people, you want them to live forever. The way to live forever is to be in a relationship with Christ. Invite people. Don't hit them over the head with your beliefs. Don't tell them they are going to hell. Don't do anything except to invite them to this relationship. Say to them, "Come and see. Come and experience Jesus." It is my goal, and it has to be your goal too. They are not my words, though; Jesus said, "Go and make disciples of all the nations." Jesus isn't only talking to Billy Graham or priests or nuns; He is talking to you!

What would be your answer if I asked you how many people you have brought to Satan? "Father!" You've brought many people to Satan. How? When you sin with others, when you tell them dirty jokes, when you get others drunk, when you have sex outside of marriage—you are taking people by the hand and saying, "Come here! I want you to know who I am following this very moment. I am following Satan, and I want you to do the same." Isn't that a nice thought!

How many people have you brought to the devil? Think about your life.

Now, think about how many people you have brought to Jesus Christ. Is there anyone that can say, "I know Jesus Christ because of (place your name here)?"

One of the questions God will ask us when we stand before Him on Judgment Day is, "Did you bring anybody with you? Where are your brothers and sisters?" Don't let your answer be, "Oh, Jesus, it was hard enough to bring myself." We have to realize that we are people on a life raft and our job is not to paddle away to safety, but to pull other people into the boat also.

I love to use the example of one of my high school students whose name is Justin Fatica. When I first started teaching at Cathedral Prep in Erie, Pennsylvania, as a brand-new teacher, I was trying to make those boys into men. I have always been a strong disciplinarian when it comes to kids. One day I was writing on the board in a class of about thirty juniors and seniors. I had been a teacher for only about a week, but I knew that I had to keep a tough control of these boys or they would eat me alive. When I turned around from the board, I saw Justin with his hands behind his head and his shoeless feet on the desk in front of him. My face was already turning a shade of crimson when I shouted, "You get your feet off that desk right now!"

Justin smiled and said, "You say 'please'."

I grabbed that little pagan and threw him out of my room. "Get the heck out of my classroom!"

He looked at me and said, "You are a jerk! It is because of people like you that nobody wants to come to Prep. You are a jerk! I am going to tell my dad."

"You tell your dad, son", I said, then, of course, I called his father first.

"I'll take care of him when he comes home, Father", Justin's dad said.

"Thank you!" I said. I love those types of fathers. They are much better than the ones who say, "Oh, what did you do to my son? Did you yell at my son?" Those kinds of fathers drive me nuts. Be a man! If I got into trouble at school, upon returning home, I would get a beating from my dad too. Nowadays, we baby our kids and claim they don't do anything wrong. That is why we raise a bunch of wimps.

Later, while I was talking to a priest friend of mine at the high school football game, Justin came right in front of me and said to Father Detisch, "Father Larry is a jerk!"

To which I responded, "You just got yourself two more hours of detention."

"I don't care", he said. "I just tell it like it is, and you are a jerk."

"You get out of my face", I said. Literally, I could not stand this kid. He was a pain in my back pew. Keep in mind: I am one of those people who take God seriously when Jesus says, "Pray for those who persecute you. Love your enemies." I take their names and I put them on a piece of paper and I pray for them.

About the same time, I was bringing the Teens Encounter Christ (TEC) retreat program to the diocese. Every day, I was praying about putting TEC together. In my prayer, God said to me, "Larry, I want you to invite Justin to make a TEC retreat."

"No," I said, "I am not inviting Justin on a TEC retreat and that is the end of it, God." For a week, I went back and forth, never once forgetting my argument with God about Justin.

"I told you to invite Justin to TEC."

"I can't stand him, God", I said. "There is no way I am inviting him to TEC." After five days of fighting with God I said, "Okay, God, I will invite him, but he is not going to come anyways."

So one day in class, I halfheartedly said, "Hey, Fatica, we are having a TEC here soon and it is going to be the first one; do you want to come on the TEC retreat?"

Justin said, "I know God already, Father. I don't need one of your retreats."

Like a smart aleck, I said, "Oh, I thought you would be able to teach us something we didn't know."

Wouldn't you know it, the little pagan showed up at our TEC retreat that weekend. As it turned out, Justin had a great conversion to Jesus on TEC. He began a relationship with Jesus Christ that lit a fire in his heart that has yet to be extinguished. When he got back to school, he started dragging freshmen in headlocks to daily Mass, practically throwing them into the chapel.

As I told you, we used to have a weekly prayer group, and Justin was part of that group. He would even lead it if I was out of town. At one of those evening prayer sessions, there were about twenty boys present; I went around and asked all the boys, "Okay, tell me how you came to know Jesus Christ." On that one night, six of the boys told me that they came to know Christ because of Justin! Justin was only a senior in high school and yet he had already been an instrument that Jesus used to bring six others to Him!

Justin graduated and went off to college, where he started his own Twelve Apostles prayer group. He told the other college students in his group, "If you want to follow Jesus Christ, then you are going to have to pray an hour a day." I thought I was tough.

He made these people pray an hour a day before the Blessed Sacrament. Since then he has started his own ministry called Hard as Nails Ministries. It has grown a lot. It has grown enough that HBO made a documentary on the life of Justin Fatica, a kid who knows Christ. He also just published a book, sharing how he brings youth to Christ all over the world.

Justin claims that I am the one who brought him to Christ. I even make an appearance in the middle of this documentary and his book. Still, I can't help remembering him as a "pain in my back pew". I am very proud of Justin. He has become a great instrument of God. You can be God's instrument too.

Like Justin's example, when we bring people to Christ, they, too, will bring others to Christ. That is how the apostles got more disciples. How will you practically bring people in your life to Christ?

I want to share with you three things that you can do to help others to get to know Christ.

The first thing you have to do to bring people to Christ is to start a list of people in your life who do not know Jesus Christ. The reason you make a list is because it helps you to focus. On my list, I make sure to include my enemies. You don't want to be selfish about this. You don't just want your family, but also that person that drives you nuts.

Abraham Lincoln once said, "I don't like that man. I must get to know him better." Likewise, Jesus calls us to love our enemies. It is not an option.

Once you have completed your list, start praying for each person by name every day. When you pray for someone, you become like a magnifying glass. You place yourself spiritually over him. Just as on a sunshiny day, when you take a magnifying glass, the rays of the sun get magnified through it and set things on fire. We are people's intercessors when we pray for them. We become the magnifying glass; then, by the grace of God, we set these people on fire with the Holy Spirit.

The second thing you must do is love the people on your list. Love them so much that you go out of your way to love them. St. Thérèse of Lisieux is a great example of going out of your way to love someone. There was someone in her order she did not like, so she went out of her way to be kinder to her. Finally, the other sister asked Thérèse, "Sister Theresa, tell me, why do you like me so much?" St. Thérèse, known as the Little Flower, did not really like the sister in her heart, but she went beyond her feelings and loved the sister anyway.

In our own lives there are people we cannot stand; we know this. That is why we need the Holy Spirit and why we need to say, "Jesus, I can't love this person, but You can through me. I will get out of the way. Love this person through me." There is a great line in a song by Steven Camp that says, "Don't tell them Jesus loves them until you are ready to love them too." We cannot share with others the love of Jesus, unless they know that we love them also.

If we want to change the world, if we want to bring others to Christ, we must love people and pray for them. We need to be kind to them. It is not our job to judge others. Yes, sometimes love has to be firm, like earlier when I talked about the boy who was living with his girlfriend. I actually saw that boy recently in Iowa where I was speaking. He brought his girlfriend with him to hear my talks. He and his girlfriend gave their lives to Christ on the last night. Blessed be God.

The difference between judging people and being strong with them is love. Pray for them. Show them that you love them, but tell them also. Then, once they know that you love them, then you can tell them about Jesus Christ.

We are told in the Gospels that people went to the disciples of Jesus and asked, "Sir, we wish to see Jesus" (Jn 12:21). When people see us, they really want to see Jesus Christ. That is why I told you to go through the Gospels and look for the characteristics of Christ that you best exemplify. Then you will be showing them a side of Christ. None of us can show all the sides of Christ, but each of us, in the Body of Christ, can show a different part. Show everybody Christ through your personality type.

The last thing that you must do to bring people to Christ is tell them about Him. Notice this is after you have prayed for them and then loved them! Keep it in this order!

And when you tell people about Christ do not preach Him to them—share Him with them. Tell them what Christ has done for you, and invite them to a relationship with Him.

Now to some of you this might sound a little like something a good Protestant would do and not a good Catholic, and that is the problem! We need to bring others to the fullness of truth about Jesus and His Church. It is His command; will you obey?

The Lord God of the universe is calling all of us to be great men, men that are examples of Him and who use Him as our example. We are called to become another Christ in this world. Our goal is to bring others to Him.

Do it and you will live forever.

Got it? Get it? Going to do it?

Good! Take courage and be a man who changes the world!

Three Tasks You Must Accomplish

1. Be a man who becomes another Christ. Spend time with Jesus reading the Gospels and write down the qualities of manhood that He possessed and ask Him to make them your own.
2. Be a man who lives God's vision for your life and the world, then live this vision with passion.

3. Be a man who changes the world one person at a time. Make a list of people you know who do not know Jesus and then pray for them and finally tell them about Jesus.

Questions for Reflection and Discussion

1. Jesus is counting on you. Are you ready? Explain.
2. Have you ever brought anyone to a relationship with Jesus? How are you going to do this in the future?
3. What do you think God's vision is for you and for the world? How are you going to implement this?

Thirty Tasks You Must Accomplish to Help You Become the Man You Were Created to Be

Okay, gentlemen. Now is the time to make sure that you put into practice what you just read! I believe that if you just read this book and nothing changes in your life, you may have wasted your time. After reading this book, you should have accomplished a total of thirty tasks—three at the end of each chapter to help you become the man you were created to be. Following is a summary listing all the "tasks that you must accomplish", with checkboxes in front of each to make sure that you have implemented these practices into your life. Make sure you do each one. So, don't be afraid—take courage and be a man!

Checklist

- [ ] 1. **Be a man who lives with your end in mind.** Write down what you want God and others to say about you when you die. These should be your new goals in life. Now set up a plan on what you need to do to reach these goals. Be practical!
- [ ] 2. **Be a man who knows God.** If you do not know God yet, then decide today that you are going to go and do whatever it takes to get to know Him. Don't wait; life is short, and eternity is forever!
- [ ] 3. **Be a man of prayer.** Commit yourself to spending at least five minutes a day with God in prayer for the rest of your life, beginning today.
- [ ] 4. **Be a man who lives as a beloved son.** Be still and let God embrace you as His son. As He spoke

to Jesus, let Him speak to you: "You are my beloved son." After spending time in His embrace, respond to Him and take five minutes to pray the "Our Father" from the depth of your being to your Father who is with you.

☐ 5. **Be a man who reads the Bible.** Decide to spend time reading Scripture every day, for it is here that God will speak to you and reveal His will to you. Live "No Bible, no breakfast; no Bible, no bed!"

☐ 6. **Be a man who listens more than he talks.** This begins with your relationship with God. Never leave your prayer time without giving time to silence.

☐ 7. **Be a man who repents.** Make a good examination of conscience and if you are Catholic make a good confession. No excuses!

☐ 8. **Be a man who fights against temptation with God's Word.** After you have discovered your core sins, look up verses in the Bible and commit them to memory so you can defeat temptations when they arise.

☐ 9. **Be a man who daily strives to grow in your manhood.** Make a nightly examination of conscience and commit yourself to go to confession at least once a month.

☐ 10. **Be a man who daily surrenders to the Holy Spirit.** Make a commitment to say a daily prayer of submission to the Holy Spirit!

☐ 11. **Be a man who uses the gifts of the Holy Spirit.** Reflect on the seven gifts of the Holy Spirit and ask God to help you to use them in your life. Take one gift each day for the next seven days and humbly ask God for that gift.

☐ 12. **Be a man who "fans into a flame" the fire of the Holy Spirit within you.** Find a friend, or a priest or a deacon, and ask him to pray over you that you would fully receive and open your heart to the gift of God's Spirit.

☐ 13. **Be a man who is strong.** Take responsibility for your life and your past. No blaming others. You got where you are because of your actions and decisions and now you can move forward with God's grace by making better decisions.

☐ 14. **Be a man who is pure of heart.** Deal with your lust by inviting Christ into the center of your struggle.

☐ 15. **Be a man of service.** Write out the words: "I am third" on a piece of paper and place it where you will see it every day, and try to live it.

☐ 16. **Be a man of generosity.** Start tithing and taking care of the poor and your parish.

☐ 17. **Be a man who tells the people you love that you love them.** Write a letter to your family members telling them how much you love them and then commit yourself to tell them that every day for the rest of your life.

☐ 18. **Be a man who loves your enemies.** Start praying for them and asking God to love them through you.

☐ 19. **Be a man who is wise.** Look at life through God's eyes and not the world's eyes. Read Philippians chapter 2. Strive to live your life this way.

☐ 20. **Be a man of obedience.** Start each day asking God what He wants and then obey Him and do it.

☐ 21. **Be a man who seeks to please God.** Too many people are concerned about what others think of them; don't be one of those people.

- [ ] 22. **Be a man who is a spiritual leader.** Take spiritual authority in your family and lead by example. Have a daily prayer time with your family.
- [ ] 23. **Be a man who needs other men.** Find men who will challenge you to grow in the Lord and make you a better man.
- [ ] 24. **Be a man who invites God into your sexuality.** If you are married, pray with your spouse, especially before sexual intimacy.
- [ ] 25. **Be a man who strives to be a saint.** Ask God for the grace to grow in your holiness.
- [ ] 26. **Be a man of devotion.** What religious practices is God calling you to start doing? Be specific and begin doing them.
- [ ] 27. **Be a man who prays and loves.** The world must know that you love the Father. This is done by praying and loving—live it.
- [ ] 28. **Be a man who becomes another Christ.** Spend time with Jesus reading the Gospels and write down the qualities of manhood that He possessed and ask Him to make them your own.
- [ ] 29. **Be a man who lives God's vision for your life and the world,** then live this vision with passion.
- [ ] 30. **Be a man who changes the world one person at a time.** Make a list of people you know who do not know Jesus and then pray for them and finally tell them about Jesus.